W9-DGE-077

NOODLES
the new way

sri owen

photographs by Gus Filgate

CONTENTS

*for Roger, Irwan, and Daniel,
my most outspoken critics –
but they all love noodles*

The basic concept of noodles is so brilliant, yet so obvious, that I have never believed the story about Marco Polo teaching the emperor of China how to make spaghetti, and then returning to Italy to show the Italians how to make noodles. I'm sure noodles and spaghetti have both been invented in different places several times over, and every time it happens there is public rejoicing.

INTRODUCTION

Considering the passion I've always had for rice, why am I writing a book about noodles? There are plenty of reasons—and I still love rice as much as ever.

Provided you have all the ingredients prepared, you can cook a one-dish gourmet meal based on noodles in less than 10 minutes. You won't find any other staple food that lets you do that and offers such a variety of accompaniments to choose from—an infinite variety, in fact, because you can go on improvising forever. Noodles, like other kinds of pasta, are mostly starch, and will absorb and set off the flavor of any sauce, or whatever else they're cooked and served with.

Noodles have another attraction for me: they are not snobs, they are at ease in any company and are perhaps the most democratic of foods. There are no right or wrong ways to eat them, just as there are no right or wrong times. They fit in anywhere. No one will mind whether you eat them elegantly, twirling them around a fork and never spilling a drop of sauce, or shovel them up with a spoon or chopsticks and end up with one long one hanging down your chin. Follow the example of Asian noodle-slurpers— tuck a few strands into your mouth with whatever tools are at hand, then suck them in powerfully, relying on the uprush of noodle to bring with it all the sauce and pieces of meat and vegetables, steaming hot.

If someone asks, "Why don't noodles come from the factory already chopped into convenient lengths?," the answer is because then they wouldn't be so much fun to eat and, therefore, wouldn't taste as good. Alternatively, give the Chinese answer—because long noodles are a symbol of long life, and cutting them short, whether in the factory, in the kitchen, or at the dinner table, might suggest long life is something we don't care about.

Cooking noodles is also very simple and almost as easy as eating them. However, a beginner can benefit from a little help and experience, and an expert remains expert by continually learning. Like any work of art, a great noodle

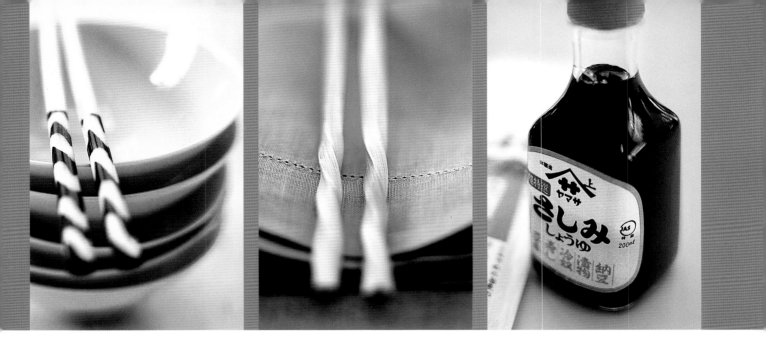

dish needs knowledge and forethought, however rapid the actual cooking may be. Your aim is to make something that combines contrasting flavors and textures in perfect harmony. The noodles themselves are, if you like, the canvas on which the picture is painted.

A Chinese or Japanese cook will say you must keep in mind the principles of yin and yang, and remember that some types of food are "hot" and others "cold." Some-one like myself, from Southeast Asia, will emphasize the balance of textures (we usually say there should be at least two, possibly three—crunchy, chewy, and soft —in a perfectly composed dish) and flavors (at least two out of the basic five—sweet, salty, hot, sour or bitter, and aromatic).

Remember that excellent Japanese movie, *Tampopo*, about a woman with the noodle bar who was determined to make perfect noodles, and was helped in this by the comments of her highly critical customers? As I watched the movie, I had the impression I could almost feel and taste every mouthful—I certainly came out hungrier than I went in.

Japanese cooks are perhaps lucky in having traditional models of what perfect noodles (and perfect anything else) ought to be. When I was younger I too paid great attention to cooking my own country's food exactly as I remembered it from my childhood in Sumatra and Java. Probably this is a

useful part of anyone's training; you learn the rules and practice them until they are second nature. Then you start to bend and break them and make something new.

In the thirty-odd years I have lived in London, Asian ingredients, flavors, and techniques have poured into restaurants, stores, and everyone's kitchens at home. It has been an exhilarating process to watch, and take part in a liberation of Western taste buds—at least for those who have not become enslaved to industrial fast food. These new resources create the need for new knowledge, the knowledge of how to use them. That is why I have devoted the past twenty years or so to writing about food—Asian food in particular—and teaching people to cook. I want my readers and my students to share my love of food, and also to understand how and why Asians cook as they do.

However, I no longer only want to re-create what is perfect or authentic from the past. The best food stores, market stalls, and supermarkets now bring us such a choice of fresh produce from so many countries that the imaginative cook may well feel like an artist who has been given a paint box full of completely new colors. All we have to do is work out the best ways to use them.

In this book, I describe and explain the basic techniques, the rules of noodle cooking. Then I show how tastes and textures from different sources can work together to make something really delicious. It's not always necessary to prepare everything from scratch; you can buy prepared and cooked ingredients that will cut cooking time, and I also give recipes and suggestions for making your own stocks, sauces, dressings, and pastes, so you don't need to have any left-over herbs go to waste or spices become dry and lose their flavor. Your refrigerator and freezer will keep you supplied with homemade mixes, ready for instant use in just the quantities you need.

By the time you have cooked your way through the recipes that follow, you will have a thorough grounding in noodle cooking, and a good basic knowledge of how ingredients are used together. If you like to "cook by the book" and take no chances, you will have a new repertoire of dishes that will be popular at all sorts of occasions and in any company. If, however, you want to strike out on your own, be a brilliant improviser at short notice, or spend an hour pondering the precise balance of smooth and crisp, sour and salty in something very simple but quite outrageous—then I hope you will find some help here as well as encouragement. Above all, remember that noodles are not just fast food, but tasty and nutritious food as well.

Main picture: fine dried egg noodles;
❶ Asian dried egg noodles;
❷ egg oil noodles;
❸ dried egg noodles in blocks.

NOODLE BASICS

First, a catalog of noodle types, arranged by the raw materials from which they are made.

Wheat flour: Chinese wheat-flour noodles (including flavored noodles and egg noodles); Japanese udon, *kishimen*, *hiyamugi*, and somen; ramen; Chinese wonton skins (round and square); egg and spring roll (*lumpia*) wrappers

Rice flour: round and flat noodles of all sizes; vermicelli; rice sticks; rice paper wrappers (Vietnamese *banh trang*, round and triangular)

Mung-bean flour: cellophane noodles

Buckwheat flour: Korean buckwheat noodles (*naengmyon*); Japanese soba and chasoba

From these, we can choose just four basic types which will be sufficient for most recipes in this book. These are the most popular and the most widely available—either in supermarkets or in Asian food stores. It is advisable to buy dry noodles, imported from the country where that particular type of noodle originated, as they will have a much better flavor and texture.

The basic types of noodle

As a general rule, if you are cooking for more than four people, or creating your own dish, allow the following quantities per person of uncooked noodles: for a first course, 2 ounces; for a main course or one-bowl meal, 3 to 4 ounces.

Cellophane noodles are the exception because they are more often used as a stuffing or a garnish than as a staple. For these, follow the exact quantities specified in the recipe.

Many stores sell noodles already shaped as the basis of stylish food presentations—"nests" are especially popular. I would not recommend buying these because, when you precook them, you will have to shake them loose, with the result that they lose their shape. If you don't do this, the noodle strands stick together and cook unevenly. Nests and baskets are fine if you want partly raw containers for your food, but I would not advise you to eat them.

EGG NOODLES—ROUND AND FLAT:
These are available in several grades, from very fine to very coarse and thick. Their country of origin is China, and they are widely exported, so buy packets of dried noodles manufactured in China.

4 Fresh flat Asian egg noodles;
5 supermarket fresh egg noodles;
6 supermarket dried egg noodles;
7 fresh fine Asian noodles.

CELLOPHANE NOODLES:

Made from mung-bean flour, these are also called glass noodles because they are almost transparent. (They may also be called bean threads, bean noodles, or cellophane vermicelli.) Don't confuse them with rice vermicelli—the raw materials are very different. Cellophane noodles do not require cooking; they simply need to be heated and softened in warm water.

RICE NOODLES:

Fine rice noodles are usually labeled as "rice vermicelli." Larger types, which can be round or flat, are called rice sticks. Those made in Vietnam or Thailand are usually of the highest quality. Because this type of noodle is made of rice flour, they are almost colorless, but opaque.

A NOTE ON FRESH RICE NOODLES:

These are usually available in Chinese food stores, near the fresh wonton skins (wrappers) and freshly made egg noodles. They are ready for immediate use in soup, or to be mixed with stir-fried vegetables and meat or shrimp. Fresh rice noodles do not need any additional cooking, but they must be reheated, which is very easy (see page 16).

Main picture: cellophane bean thread noodles;
❶ round rice noodles;
❷ wide ribbon rice sticks;
❸ narrow ribbon rice sticks;
❹ rice vermicelli.

JAPANESE NOODLES:

These are further subdivided into three types:

Soba noodles, which are made with 80 to 90 percent buckwheat flour (the rest is wheat flour), giving them a slightly brown color. Buckwheat flour by itself would make the noodles too brittle. Look for them, neatly cut into sticks about 8 inches long, packed in Japan, and labeled entirely in Japanese. If the label is entirely or partly in English, the contents have probably not been made for the Japanese market. In that case, they may not be of the highest standard, and they may contain a higher proportion of wheat flour than those made in Japan.

Udon, which are usually fat, round noodles, white in color, and made of wheat flour and water. Flat udon are sometimes available.

Somen, which are fine white noodles made from wheat flour and water, with a little oil. Packed in neat bundles (if they are imported from Japan, they are often tied with colorful ribbons), they are available from most Japanese stores, but rarely from elsewhere. Like soba, they are often served cold with a dipping sauce.

Main picture: soba noodles;
❺ reconstituted udon noodles;
❻ round udon noodles;
❼ flat udon noodles;
❽ somen noodles.

Main picture: triangular rice paper;

❶ round wonton skins;
❷ square wonton skins;
❸ egg roll wrappers.

The basic types of wrapper

Four types of wrapper will be enough to fit the needs of the recipes featured in this book. These wrappers are the most popular and the most widely available—either in supermarkets or in Asian food stores.

RICE PAPERS (VIETNAMESE *BANH TRANG*):

These are not the rolled sheets of edible paper that pastries such as macaroons are baked on. These are stiff and very brittle, so they need careful handling. They are sold dry, usually in clear plastic packages, and come in several sizes, but only in two shapes—circles and triangles. The circles, which are the ones I most often use, can be bought in at least three sizes: small (6 inches in diameter), medium (8 inches), and large (11½ inches).

Before use, rice papers must be softened. To do this, immerse them, one sheet at a time, in a bowl of warm water, and in less than a minute, they become soft and pliable. Lift the sheet out carefully—it will tear easily—and lay it flat on a tray. Dab away the excess water with paper towels, then arrange the filling or stuffing on top of it, and roll it up (see the recipe for Vietnamese Rice Paper Rolls on page 130.)

Filled rolls can be deep-fried or steamed. Be careful not to make any tear in the rice paper if it is to be fried, because even a small hole will let the oil get inside. If rice papers are used as wrappers for food that has already been cooked, or for fresh raw vegetables and salad leaves, then the papers themselves must be softened in hot (but not boiling) water. This will not only soften the paper but heat it sufficiently to cook it.

EGG ROLL WRAPPERS:

These are usually available in freezers in Chinese and many other Asian food stores. They are square and come in three sizes: 5 inches, 10 inches, and 12 inches. The dough dries out very quickly if it gets a chance, so the best way to work with them is to thaw a whole package and carefully peel off the wrappers one by one. The ones you don't use can then be refrozen. Once the sheets have been separated, they stay separate and you can fill and roll them quickly, even after they have been refrozen.

WONTON SKINS:

You can buy these fresh or frozen, usually in packages of 6 to 8 ounces, or in larger packages about twice this weight. They are very thin dough squares, about 3 inches on each side, but you can also buy round ones, about the same diameter. Both shapes are available thin, for frying, or slightly thicker for steaming. Because they are made with eggs, wonton skins (of whatever shape) don't stick to each other.

how to cook the basic types of noodles

There are essentially just two or three simple stages in the cooking of most types of noodles, all of them very short and simple—precooking (usually followed by refreshing) and reheating or additional cooking.

For perfect results (tender but still firm), noodles must first be precooked for the correct length of time, then refreshed under cold running water—to stop more cooking—until cold. They are then reheated or cooked again, as required. Cooking can, if required, be done some time before the noodles are to be eaten, but preferably not more than one hour ahead.

Some types of noodle, if left in a colander more than half an hour, will cling together and form a solid lump. Others, especially best-quality noodles, can be refreshed and left to drain for up to an hour, yet still remain separate.

If you want to shape or arrange your noodles, or make them lie straight on the plate or fold them over, the time to do this is immediately after precooking. As long as you are reasonably careful when you reheat them, they will keep the shape you gave them. This way you can style them for an attractive presentation, arranged to suit the other ingredients.

Precooking noodles
EGG NOODLES:
Half-fill a large saucepan with water and bring to a boil. Add 1 teaspoon salt and adjust the heat to keep the water at a rolling boil. Add the noodles and use long bamboo chopsticks or a fork to move the noodles about so the bundles loosen and separate. Cook for 2½ to 3 minutes.

Transfer the noodles to a colander and hold them under cold running water, agitating them gently with your fingers so they stay separate and the whole mass cools quickly and completely. Leave them in the colander to drain.

RICE NOODLES:
Rice sticks, or wide ribbon-type rice noodles, should be cooked and then refreshed under cold running water as egg noodles. Fine rice noodles, or rice vermicelli, need only to be soaked in a pan or bowl of hot but not boiling water. Make sure the noodles are completely immersed, cover, and leave for 6 to 8 minutes. Drain them, put them under cold running water for 2 minutes, and drain again.

SOBA NOODLES, UDON, SOMEN:
Cook these as you would cook egg noodles, but without salt. Soba and somen should be boiled for 2 to 2½ minutes only; udon for 3 to 3½ minutes. (If you cook Japanese noodles the Japanese way as below, which involves adding cold water three times during cooking, the whole process will take up to 5 minutes.) Refresh under cold running water as described for egg noodles.

CELLOPHANE NOODLES OR CELLOPHANE VERMICELLI:
Put the noodles in a large bowl and cover them completely with hot water from a kettle that has boiled and then been left to stand for 5 minutes. Leave the noodles under the hot water for 5 to 8 minutes. Drain them, refresh under cold running water, and drain them again.

THE JAPANESE WAY:
For soba and fine egg noodles, as well as for somen (the fine Japanese wheat-flour noodles), the Japanese cooking technique insures the noodles do not become too soft through overcooking. Half-fill a pan with water and bring to a boil. Add the noodles, leave them in the boiling water for 1 minute, then add 1 cup cold water. Bring the water back to a boil and boil slowly for 1 minute longer, then add a second cup of cold water. Repeat this cycle once more: 1 minute boiling, then add one third cup of cold water. Taste a short piece of noodle: it should still be firm, but taste cooked. (I have found that noodles cooked this way require a total cooking time of 5 minutes.) Drain, and refresh under cold running water. There is usually no need to add salt at this stage.

Refreshing precooked noodles under cold running water until they are very cold stops additional cooking and reduces the chance of them sticking together.

Reheating noodles

Noodles cooked as described on page 14 need to be reheated before serving, unless (as sometimes happens) the recipe instructs you otherwise. The following are the simplest methods of reheating:

If you are preparing and cooking noodles for two people only, simply put the precooked noodles into a strainer (a conical sieve, if you like, but any shape will do) and pour a kettleful of boiling water over the noodles in a steady stream that should last up to 30 seconds. This will loosen any bundle of cold, precooked noodles, heating them at the same time. Give the strainer a good shake to drain off all the water. Arrange the noodles on plates or in bowls, or stir-fry them, according to the recipe.

If you are cooking noodles for four people or more, the easiest way to reheat them is in a large saucepan of boiling water. The water should be actually boiling when you plunge the strainer containing the noodles into it. Keep the noodles submerged for 20 seconds, no more. Lift them out, give the strainer a shake to drain the noodles well, and continue with the recipe.

Storing uncooked and cooked noodles

Fresh noodles should, obviously, be cooked and eaten as soon as possible, but what about packages of dried noodles? Once you have opened the package, should you cook all of them or can you keep some of them uncooked for a few days or weeks? This really depends on how the noodles were packed. Straight noodles, that are easily separated, can be kept in a zip-lock bag or a glass jar for up to a day. Noodles that are packed in a skein or a tangled mass are usually impossible to separate neatly, and once the package is opened they should all be cooked together.

Cooked noodles should, ideally, be eaten as fresh as possible. If you have cooked far more than people can eat, however, the leftovers will keep perfectly well in a covered bowl in the refrigerator for at least a week, and can be reheated and served again in almost any of the dishes described in this book.

I would not, of course, serve leftover noodles to my guests, but I'm not sure they would notice if I did, and I eat them myself with enjoyment.

making noodles at home

It is always a pleasure to make things by hand—up to a point. The only tools you really need for making fresh noodles are a rolling pin, a sharp knife, and a ruler. A pasta machine does make the job quicker, however, and the noodles are perhaps a little more even in width and thickness.

Wheat-flour egg noodles   Serves 4 to 6

1½ tablespoons salt
1 egg yolk
4¾ cups plus 1 tablespoon all-purpose flour, plus more for dusting

1 In a bowl, dissolve the salt in 1 cup cold water by stirring it with a fork. Add the egg yolk and beat the mixture until everything is well blended.

2 Sift the flour onto a work surface or into a large bowl and make a well in the center. Pour in the water and egg mixture, a little at a time. As you pour, mix the flour and the liquid slowly with the other hand to make a dough (you may not need all the egg mix).

3 Then, with both hands, knead the dough vigorously until it is smooth and firm. Use the heel of one hand to push the dough firmly across the work surface, then roll it up and work it with both hands to get rid of creases and air bubbles. This kneading will take about 8 minutes.

4 Put the dough into a bowl and cover with a damp dish towel. Leave in a cool place (not in the refrigerator) for 2 to 3 hours.

5 On a floured work surface, roll out one quarter of the dough to make a thin, more or less rectangular, sheet. This rolling will take some time and effort—the dough by now will be very elastic.

6 Once the dough has been rolled out thinly and evenly, leave it for 30 seconds or so to dry a little, then sprinkle a little flour over the surface. Fold the sheet to make three equal layers. Then, at right angles to the folds, cut the dough into strips, using a plastic ruler as a guide. The width of the strips may vary from very narrow to ½ inch or even 1 inch wide, according to your preference and how you intend to cook the noodles. Repeat this process until all the dough has been rolled, folded, and cut.

7 Spread out the noodles on a large tray and leave them to dry for 5 to 10 minutes. Cook the noodles in plenty of boiling water, as described in How to Cook the Basic Types of Noodles on page 14.

Making wheat-flour egg noodles: ❶ Mix the flour and egg gently to make a dough. ❷ Using the heel of your hand, knead the dough firmly across the work surface until it is smooth and firm.

❸ Roll up the dough and work with both hands to eliminate creases and air bubbles. ❹ After resting, rolling, and brief drying, fold into three and cut across into strips. ❺ Spread out the noodles and leave them to dry.

Soba (buckwheat) noodles

If you have a pasta machine and a little experience of making pasta, you will have no difficulty making soba. Even if you don't have a machine, you can roll out, fold, and cut the dough as described for wheat-flour egg noodles opposite. You do, however, need to use Japanese buckwheat flour. Serves 4 to 6

1 extra-large egg
3½ cups sifted Japanese buckwheat flour
1 cup plus 1½ tablespoons all-purpose flour, plus more for dusting

❶ Whisk the egg in a bowl, add 1 cup cold water, and whisk again.
❷ Combine both flours in a bowl. Sift them into another bowl, then put the sifted flour into a food processor. With the machine running, slowly pour just enough of the egg-and-water mixture into the flour to form a dough.
❸ Transfer this dough to a bowl and knead it for a minute or so. Divide the dough into six pieces and roll each piece into a small ball. Leave the balls to rest under an upturned bowl for about 30 minutes.
❹ Put a ball of dough into a pasta machine and roll it to make a thin sheet. Repeat this process until you have six sheets of dough. Put each sheet through the cutter. Hang the cut noodles to dry for a few minutes, just as you would if you were making Italian pasta. Cook the noodles as described on page 14.

basic stocks

As in most cuisines, good stock forms the basis of a wide range of soups and sauces. Fresh stocks are increasingly available commercially, but nothing can beat the flavor of a homemade stock—and they are so inexpensive and easy to make.

Dashi

This Japanese stock made from dried bonito (tuna) forms the basis for most Japanese soups. Japanese food stores sell instant dashi, which is good but not as good as the fresh homemade product. Once you have found kelp (*konbu*) and dried bonito flakes (*katsuobushi*), the rest is easy. **Makes about 1¼ quarts**

1 piece of kelp, about 2 inches long
4 tablespoons bonito flakes

❶ Put the kelp into a saucepan with about 4 cups water. Bring almost to a boil.
❷ Take out the kelp and bring the water to a boil. Add ½ cup cold water and the bonito flakes.
❸ Bring the water back to a boil, then immediately take the pan off the heat. Let it stand for 30 seconds. Strain the stock through a strainer lined with cheesecloth.
❹ Use the stock as directed in recipes. It can be stored, in a covered bowl, in the refrigerator for up to a week.

Basic fish stock

Use any white fish heads, bones, and trimmings, with the addition of one small whole fish—a flounder, for example. For a stronger stock, add about 9 ounces of well-washed shrimp shells near the end of cooking. **Makes about 1¼ quarts**

about 2 pounds head, bones, and trimmings of white fish
1 small whole fish, such as flounder
1 onion, sliced
1 celery stalk, coarsely chopped
½ teaspoon salt
½ pound shrimp shells (optional)

❶ Put all the ingredients, except the shrimp shells if using, in a large saucepan with 1½ to 2 quarts cold water. Bring to a boil and simmer slowly for 20 to 25 minutes.
❷ If you are using shrimp shells, add them now, with an additional ½ cup water. Bring the stock back to a boil and simmer for 10 minutes longer.
❸ Strain the stock and leave it to cool. Store in the refrigerator for 8 to 10 days, until needed.

Plainly cooked egg noodles in a tasty and nourishing vegetable stock (overleaf), make a simple but satisfying soup.

Basic miso stock

This can be used as a base for many different noodle soups. It is important that the stock is perfectly clear and not have too many contrasting flavors. Therefore, the other ingredients of the noodle soup must not overpower the stock, and vice versa. Each ingredient should retain its own flavor, distinct from the others, but not drowning them. **Makes about 1¾ quarts**

1 shallot, chopped
1 garlic clove, chopped
½-inch slice gingerroot
2 tablespoons rice (or barley) and soybean miso (page 141)

❶ Put all the ingredients in a large saucepan with 2¼ quarts cold water. Bring to a boil and simmer, uncovered, for 1 to 2 hours.
❷ Strain the stock through a strainer lined with cheesecloth or paper towels. Be patient—it will take a long time to strain through.
❸ Cover the bowl. The stock can now be stored in the refrigerator, and will stay fresh for 7 to 10 days. Use as directed in your chosen recipe.

Basic Asian stock

This is how basic nonmeat stock is made for Thai cooking. If you wish, you can add vegetables to make a basic vegetable stock: the quantities of water and salt are the same whether or not you add extra vegetables. If you do add vegetables, you will need to let the stock simmer for a total of 40 to 50 minutes.
Makes about 1¾ quarts

3 shallots, coarsely chopped
1 lemongrass stalk, cut across into 3 pieces
1-inch piece galangal (page 140), sliced
1 large red chili, seeded and split lengthwise into two pieces (optional)
½ teaspoon salt

❶ Put all the ingredients into a large saucepan with 2 quarts cold water. Bring to a boil and simmer slowly for 20 to 25 minutes, skimming from time to time.
❷ Strain the stock into a bowl and leave to cool; discard the solids. Store in the refrigerator for up to 10 days until needed.
Variation for basic vegetable stock: Add other vegetables, such as carrots, celery, or a potato or two, to this Thai stock and it becomes a basic vegetable stock that can be used in recipes with no connection whatever with Thailand. The only preparation such vegetables require is cutting into large chunks. Just put them in the pan with the other ingredients and simmer for an additional 20 to 25 minutes—that is, 40 to 50 minutes altogether. Strain the stock and store as described above.

Basic chicken stock

For best results, use the whole chicken—a free-range bird if possible. Cut it lengthwise into halves and wash the inside cavity very thoroughly. Discard any remains of the variety meat and giblets clinging to the bones, otherwise the stock will taste bitter. Makes about 2 quarts

1 whole chicken, preferably free-range
1 large onion, cut into quarters (the onion skin can go in as well, if you like)
1 teaspoon salt

❶ With a sharp knife, cut the two pieces of breast meat from the breastbone. Put the two halves of the carcass and the two pieces of breast meat in a large saucepan. Pour in enough cold water to cover the meat and the carcass, about 2½ quarts. Add the onion and salt and bring the water to a boil. Lower the heat so the water temperature is just above simmering point. This is important, because at this temperature the froth will rise to the surface and you can skim it off.

❷ When the stock has been simmering for 20 minutes, take out the 2 pieces of breast meat with a draining spoon; set aside. When they are cool enough to handle, they can be sliced very thinly and used in the following recipes: Laksa Lemak on page 72; Indonesian Chicken Soup with Rice Noodles on page 87; and Egg Noodles with Chicken and Shiitake Mushrooms on page 90.

❸ The rest of the chicken should be left simmering for about 2 hours longer. Add more cold water from time to time to replace what has evaporated and, of course, you should skim the froth from the surface from time to time.

❹ After 2 hours of simmering, remove the pan from the heat. Let the stock cool a little, then strain it through a fine-meshed strainer into a large bowl. The carcass should now be thrown away (the meat that is still on it has no flavor and is not worth eating).

❺ The stock, when cool, can be stored in the refrigerator. Next day, skim off and discard the fat that has hardened on the surface. The stock can now be kept in the refrigerator until needed; it will keep perfectly well for at least 5 days. This stock can also be frozen in an ice-cube tray, and will keep in the freezer for up to 3 months.

Beef stock

I find the best-tasting beef stock is made with brisket. **Makes about 6¾ quarts**

3 pounds beef brisket, cut into about 6 pieces
1 teaspoon salt

❶ Put the meat and salt in a large saucepan with 3¼ quarts cold water. Bring to a boil, lower the heat, and simmer, letting the water just bubble, for 1 hour. Skim off the froth from time to time.

❷ After 1 hour, add more water to bring it back up to its original level and bring it back to a boil. Lower the heat and continue to simmer for 2 hours longer.

❸ Let the stock cool a little and then strain it through a strainer lined with cheesecloth into a large bowl. Cover and refrigerate, then discard the fat that solidifies on the surface of the stock.

❹ Use the stock as required. The pieces of beef can be used in a casserole if you wish, but they have very little flavor left in them.

dipping sauces

I have collected or created several dipping sauces, starting
with the mild Japanese original and progressing to some
eclectic and spicier ones. When the recipe specifies a
number it will serve, such as "Serves 4 to 6," this
amount is "one measure." A few recipes require
more than this. Noodles with a dipping
sauce are usually served as a light
one-bowl lunch throughout Asia.

Beet and anchovy dipping sauce

The method of cooking beets here is taken from Christopher Lloyd's *Gardener Cook*. He says the best way is to put the beets on a baking tray with the oven set at 300°F and roast for 1 to 1½ hours for small beets, or 2 to 3 hours for large ones.

As with homemade pickles and chutneys, this dip will keep in airtight jars in the refrigerator for up to two weeks, possibly a little longer. Like the Spicy Avocado Dipping Sauce (page 30), it can be eaten with cold soba noodles or any other kind of cold, warm, or hot noodle. You can also use it as a dressing for hot egg noodles.

Makes about 2½ cups

1 pound young whole beets, cooked as above
4 to 6 ounces canned anchovies in olive oil, drained and chopped
2 shallots, finely chopped
1 garlic clove, crushed
1 teaspoon finely chopped gingerroot
2 to 6 bird's-eye chilies, seeded and finely chopped
2 tablespoons finely chopped parsley
3 tablespoons white-wine vinegar or Japanese brown rice vinegar
1 tablespoon extra-virgin olive oil
2 teaspoons brown sugar
a pinch of salt or ½ teaspoon fish sauce (*nam pla*, page 140)

❶ The skins of the cooked beets can be peeled off with your fingers, under cold running water if you prefer. Dice the peeled beets very small, and put in a glass serving bowl.

❷ Add all the other ingredients and blend well with a fork. Leave at room temperature for 30 minutes.

❸ Taste and adjust the seasoning: the flavor should be hot, sour, and slightly sweet. The dip can be served immediately.

❹ For storage, transfer the dip to a jar with an airtight lid, and keep it in the refrigerator for up to 14 days.

Japanese dipping sauce

My first encounter with cold noodles took place when I was in Hiroshima in 1991. I had been told that the weather in Japan in July and August is so hot that soba noodles and somen are often served cold or even chilled on ice.

In a noodle bar next to the railroad station, I pointed to a picture of soba noodles beautifully presented in a basket. Accompanying them was a bowl of dipping sauce. The food was served, and I found I did not care for it at all—probably because I wasn't expecting noodles to be cold. Even in tropical Java, we had been brought up on piping hot noodle soup or fried noodles. However, when a Japanese friend invited me to her home and served me more cold soba noodles with dipping sauce I enjoyed them very much; so, if they are an acquired taste, at least the taste is acquired quickly. **Makes about 2½ cups**

2 tablespoons dried bonito flakes (page 140) or 2 tablespoons dried shrimp
2½ cups Dashi (page 21)
⅔ cup dark soy sauce
3 tablespoons mirin (page 141)
½ teaspoon sugar

❶ If using bonito flakes, put all the ingredients except the bonito flakes into a saucepan and bring the mixture to a boil. Add the bonito flakes immediately and take the pan off the heat. Leave the bonito flakes to steep in the liquid for 20 to 30 seconds. Strain the sauce and discard the solids.

❷ If using dried shrimp, soak them in boiling water for 5 minutes, then drain them, discarding the soaking water. Put the soaked shrimp into a saucepan and add all the other ingredients. Bring this mixture to a boil and take it off the heat. Let the sauce cool a little, then strain it and discard the solids.

❸ Let the dipping sauce cool to room temperature before serving. In an airtight jar, this can be stored in the refrigerator for up to 1 month.

Spicy avocado dipping sauce

Avocado trees grow prolifically in the tropics. There was a large one in my parents' garden, producing enormous quantities of fruit, but we never thought of eating the avocados as a savory—my mother had learned from Dutch books and from her Dutch friends that they should be made into mousse for dessert. I hated this mousse, because it was always made with canned condensed milk and contained far more sugar than was good for me.

Now, however, Indonesians have realized that avocado with plenty of chilies and lime juice makes an excellent dip for serving with crudités and cooked shrimp. In this book, I am introducing it as a dipping sauce for cold soba noodles, or indeed for any kind of noodle—cold, warm, or hot. **Serves 4**

2 to 3 tablespoons lime juice (about 2 limes)
2 teaspoons brown sugar
½ teaspoon sea salt
2 to 4 bird's-eye chilies, chopped
2 garlic cloves, finely chopped
1 or 2 ripe avocados

❶ Mix all the ingredients except the avocado in a glass bowl.
❷ When you are ready to serve, peel and dice the avocados. Mix them well with the other ingredients.
❸ Divide between four bowls and serve.

Rujak sauce

This piquant sauce is very popular in Indonesia and Malaysia, where people use it mainly to dress salads of sour fruit. Recently, however, many Asian chefs have begun to use it as a sauce for steaks and other broiled meats. Here, I recommend it as a spicy dipping sauce for cold soba noodles.
Serves 4 (makes about ½ cup)

4 tablespoons hot water
½ cup packed grated palm sugar or soft brown sugar
½ teaspoon broiled shrimp paste (page 141)
2 tablespoons lime juice or tamarind water (page 142)
1 teaspoon salt
2 to 4 bird's-eye chilies, finely chopped
4 scallions, thinly sliced (optional)

❶ Mix everything except the scallions in a glass bowl, stirring to dissolve the sugar, shrimp paste, and salt.
❷ Divide between four small bowls and scatter with the sliced scallions, if using.

Soy sauce with chilies

This is widely used in Indonesia and Malaysia—not, in fact, as a dipping sauce for noodles (the way the Japanese prefer), but as a dip for egg rolls and crudités, and to add flavor and hotness to noodle and rice dishes. **Makes about 6 tablespoons**

4 tablespoons light or dark soy sauce
2 to 6 bird's-eye chilies, finely chopped
1 shallot, finely chopped
1 tablespoon lime or lemon juice
1 teaspoon sugar (if light soy is used)

❶ Mix all the ingredients together in a small bowl.
❷ Use as needed; this will keep in the refrigerator for up to 7 days.

Nuoc cham (fish sauce with chilies)

Instead of soy sauce, the peoples of Thailand, Vietnam, Cambodia, Laos—and, to some extent, Burma—prefer fish sauce. Called *nam pla* (page 141) in Thailand, *nuoc mam* in Vietnam, the combination of ingredients is generally the same as for Soy Sauce with Chilies (above), except in the typical Vietnamese dipping sauce, *nuoc cham*. **Serves 6 to 8**

4 tablespoons fish sauce
2 tablespoons lime or lemon juice
2 to 6 bird's-eye chilies, chopped
1 or 2 garlic cloves, crushed
1 small carrot, grated
1 to 2 tablespoons chopped cilantro leaves

❶ Combine the fish sauce, lime or lemon juice, chilies, and garlic in a small bowl. Cover the bowl and refrigerate until 1 to 2 hours before serving.
❷ Add the grated carrots and chopped cilantro leaves and refrigerate again until the moment the sauce goes to the table. (Once the carrots and cilantro leaves have been added, the sauce must be consumed on the same day.)

Basic chili sauce

I include this under the heading of Dipping Sauces because most people in Southeast Asia like to dip almost everything they eat in chili sauce, from raw vegetables and egg rolls to meat, fish, cooked vegetables, rice, and noodles. Because this habit has now spread to the West, we can buy bottled chili sauces in Asian grocery stores and most supermarkets.

The one most widely available is probably *sambal ulek,* which Dutch producers still spell in the old way, "*sambal oelek*." This is not a brand name, but a description of the sauce, the vital ingredient of which is mashed and pounded chilies. The stuff you buy in shops is good—I often buy it myself—but you can make your own, which is at least as good and costs much less.

Chili sauce can also be used in cooking. If the recipe requires, say, two or three chilies to be blended with other ingredients to make a spice paste, their place can be taken by 1 tablespoonful of this sauce. **Makes about 2 cups**

½ to 1 pound large fresh red chilies
1 to 1½ teaspoons salt
3 tablespoons peanut oil
1 tablespoon distilled white vinegar or tamarind water (page 142)

❶ Put the chilies in a large pan of boiling water and cook for 2 minutes; drain.
❷ Transfer the chilies to a blender, add the other ingredients, and blend to the smoothest possible paste.
❸ Transfer this to a saucepan and cook over low heat for 10 to 12 minutes, stirring occasionally. Take great care, because the liquid will bubble and spit as it cooks.
❹ Leave the sauce to cool completely before storing in an airtight jar: it will keep in the refrigerator for 3 weeks or longer.

❶ Cook the chilies in boiling water for 2 minutes. ❷ After blending, cook the chili mixture slowly for 10 to 12 minutes. (Take care because it will bubble and spit.) ❸ Leave the sauce to cool before storing in an airtight jar.

dressings

All the dressings in this section are intended to dress cellophane noodles, served with whatever additional ingredients the various recipes include. Alternatively, the dressings can be used with plain noodles or salads.

Piquant Thai dressing

Thais use more chilies than here; it's a matter of taste. "Piquant" signifies "CHILI HOT." However, this version isn't too hot, even for those unaccustomed to chilies. I use it for all kinds of salad, whenever I want an oil-free dressing. Serves 4

2 bird's-eye chilies, finely chopped
2 scallions, thinly sliced
2 tablespoons chopped cilantro leaves
2 tablespoons chopped lemongrass (the inner part only)
1 teaspoon grated palm sugar or soft brown sugar
2 to 3 tablespoons fish sauce (*nam pla*, page 140)
4 tablespoons lime juice

❶ Mix all the ingredients in a glass bowl.
❷ Cover and refrigerate until needed, up to 4 or 5 days.

Piquant dressing with crushed peanuts

Thais love peanuts in salad dressings, not just for their flavor, but to add another texture. In fact, they use peanuts in much the same way as Mediterranean cooks use pine nuts. Serves 4

2 tablespoons fish sauce (*nam pla*, page 140)
2 to 4 bird's-eye chilies (red or green), finely chopped
4 tablespoons lime or lemon juice
1 or 2 garlic cloves, crushed
1 to 2 teaspoons finely chopped gingerroot
1 to 2 teaspoons brown sugar or grated palm sugar
½ to 1 cup Garlic-flavored fried peanuts (page 45), or any store-bought roasted peanuts, crushed

❶ Mix all the ingredients except the peanuts in a glass bowl. Cover and refrigerate until needed (up to a week).
❷ The crushed nuts are sprinkled over the whole salad or noodle dish served with this dressing. Do this just before serving, so they stay crunchy.

Tofu dressing

This dressing also contains sesame-seed paste. For best results, make this paste yourself as below, but you can, of course, buy sesame-seed paste from Asian grocery stores. Be warned, however, that these contain peanuts. The Middle Eastern paste, tahina, can be used instead for this recipe. **Serves 4–6**

2 tablespoons mirin (page 141)
1 tablespoon soft brown sugar
1 teaspoon salt
3 tablespoons Dashi (page 21) or other stock
1 block Japanese "cotton" or "firm silken" tofu
2 bird's-eye chilies, finely chopped (optional)
1 tablespoon light soy sauce
2 to 3 teaspoons lime juice or lemon juice

for the sesame-seed paste:
1½ to 3 cups sesame seeds

❶ First make the sesame-seed paste if using your own: dry-fry the seeds in a skillet over medium heat, stirring constantly, for about 3 minutes or until golden brown. Tip out of the pan and leave to cool.
❷ When cool, pour the seeds into a blender and blend to a smooth paste—just until it becomes a little oily.
❸ Press this through a strainer if you want your paste to be really smooth. (This is hard work, and you will lose a lot of paste as it sticks to the mesh of the strainer—I prefer my paste slightly coarse anyway.) Keep the paste in an airtight jar in the refrigerator until needed, up to 7 days.
❹ Heat the mirin in a small saucepan for 2 minutes. Add the sugar, salt, and stock, stirring to dissolve the sugar and salt. Turn off the heat and leave to cool a little.
❺ When the liquid is cool, pour it into a blender and add the rest of the ingredients, except the lime or lemon juice, with 2 tablespoons of the sesame-seed paste and blend until smooth.
❻ Transfer the mixture to a glass bowl, cover and refrigerate until needed. Before use, stir the paste with a fork and add 2 to 3 teaspoons lime or lemon juice to get the right consistency and to sharpen the flavor.

Spicy coconut dressing

Although coconuts are not used for cooking in Japan, Korea, or northern China—least of all with noodles—I cannot leave out this dressing. After all, the recipes in this book come from many parts of the globe, and a lot of them use coconut milk, so I recommend you try coconut as a dressing, too. Serves 4 to 6

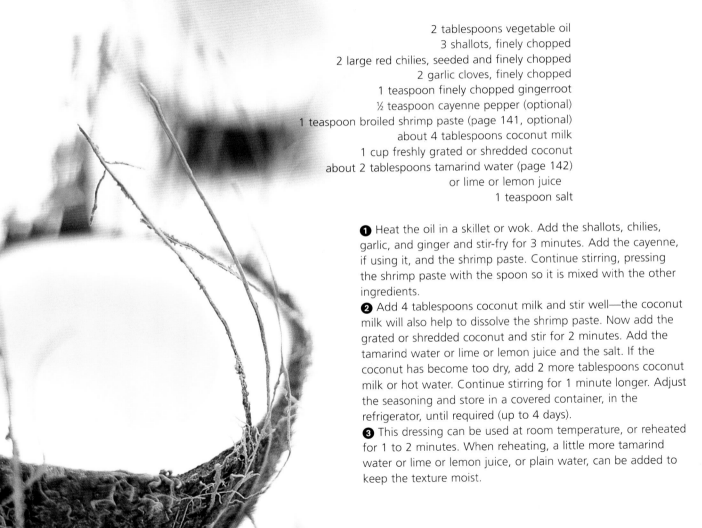

2 tablespoons vegetable oil
3 shallots, finely chopped
2 large red chilies, seeded and finely chopped
2 garlic cloves, finely chopped
1 teaspoon finely chopped gingerroot
½ teaspoon cayenne pepper (optional)
1 teaspoon broiled shrimp paste (page 141, optional)
about 4 tablespoons coconut milk
1 cup freshly grated or shredded coconut
about 2 tablespoons tamarind water (page 142)
or lime or lemon juice
1 teaspoon salt

❶ Heat the oil in a skillet or wok. Add the shallots, chilies, garlic, and ginger and stir-fry for 3 minutes. Add the cayenne, if using it, and the shrimp paste. Continue stirring, pressing the shrimp paste with the spoon so it is mixed with the other ingredients.

❷ Add 4 tablespoons coconut milk and stir well—the coconut milk will also help to dissolve the shrimp paste. Now add the grated or shredded coconut and stir for 2 minutes. Add the tamarind water or lime or lemon juice and the salt. If the coconut has become too dry, add 2 more tablespoons coconut milk or hot water. Continue stirring for 1 minute longer. Adjust the seasoning and store in a covered container, in the refrigerator, until required (up to 4 days).

❸ This dressing can be used at room temperature, or reheated for 1 to 2 minutes. When reheating, a little more tamarind water or lime or lemon juice, or plain water, can be added to keep the texture moist.

pastes

Spicy curry pastes not only form the basis
of many flavorful dishes, but they may
be used as dipping sauces for cold or hot
noodles, or even to flavor stir-fries.

Red curry paste

For the best curry pastes, you need to dry-roast or dry-fry the coriander and cumin seeds before blending them with the other ingredients. Do this in a skillet or wok, over medium heat, stirring the seeds constantly, for about 3 minutes. Don't let them burn, or they will taste bitter.

The quantities shown here will make about 2¹/₂ cups of curry paste, a good deal more than you are likely to need at one time. The surplus can be frozen in an ice-cube tray (2 tablespoons to each cube) and frozen for up to 3 months; the cubes are ready for use any time as instant curry paste. Alternatively, the paste will keep fresh in the refrigerator for 7 to 10 days in an airtight jar. **Makes about 2½ cups**

5 to 10 large red chilies, seeded and chopped
1 red bell pepper, seeded and chopped (optional)
8 shallots, chopped
8 garlic cloves, chopped
1 lemongrass stalk (inner part only), chopped
½-inch piece galangal (page 140), peeled and chopped
3 kaffir lime leaves, shredded (optional)

3 tablespoons roasted coriander seeds, crushed
1 tablespoon roasted cumin seeds, crushed
3 tablespoons tamarind water (page 142), or lime or lemon juice
3 tablespoons vegetable oil
1 teaspoon salt
1 teaspoon brown sugar

❶ Put all the ingredients in a blender with ½ cup cold water and blend until smooth.

❷ Transfer the mixture to a saucepan over high heat. Bring to a boil, lower the heat, and simmer slowly for 40 minutes.

❸ Leave the paste to cool completely, then store it in a covered jar in the refrigerator for up to 10 days until required. Alternatively, freeze the paste in ice-cube trays as described above. Transfer the frozen cubes to a plastic bag and keep frozen until needed.

Green curry paste

This classic Thai green curry paste is a very versatile mixture, which is particularly useful if you keep it frozen in ice-cube trays as described for Red Curry Paste on the previous page. You can use it as a dipping sauce for cold or hot noodles, to flavor stir-fried vegetables (see the recipe on page 54), or simply to make a traditional Thai green curry with chicken, or with shrimp or lobster, to be eaten accompanied by plain rice noodles. **Makes about 2½ cups**

6 tablespoons coriander seeds
2 tablespoons cumin seeds
10 garlic cloves, chopped
1-inch piece peeled galangal (page 140), finely chopped
2 tablespoons peanut or vegetable oil
4 to 6 green chilies, chopped
2 green bell peppers, seeded and chopped
1½ cups chopped shallots
2 teaspoons shrimp paste (page 141)
4-ounce bunch cilantro (including leaves, roots and stems), trimmed and chopped
2 lemongrass stalks (inner parts only), chopped
juice of 2 limes, about 3 or 4 tablespoons
2 teaspoons sea salt

1 Roast the coriander and cumin seeds in a dry skillet over medium heat, stirring constantly, until they are just becoming brown and fragrant.

2 Put the roasted seeds into a food processor together with the garlic cloves, chopped galangal, and oil and process for 1 minute. Add the remaining ingredients with 4 tablespoons water and process for 3 minutes to make a smooth, free-flowing paste.

3 Transfer the paste to a saucepan. Heat to just below a boil and simmer slowly for 5 to 8 minutes, stirring often. Add 1¼ cups hot water and bring to a boil. Cover the pan and simmer slowly for 40 minutes, until the paste is very thick but still flows freely.

4 The paste is now ready to use, or to be cooled and then stored in the refrigerator or freezer as described for the Red Curry Paste on the previous page.

Stages in making and storing curry pastes:
1 Process all the ingredients together for 1 minute, then add a little water and process for 2 or 3 minutes more until you have a smooth, free-flowing paste. **2** Transfer to a saucepan and cook over very low heat for about 40 minutes. **3** Leave the paste to cool completely in the pan, then store in the refrigerator or pour it into ice-cube trays for freezing in convenient 2-tablespoon blocks.

Paste for laksa

The name "laksa" is understood everywhere now to mean a spicy noodle soup made with coconut milk. The original dish, from Malaysia, is called laksa lemak, meaning "delicious laksa" or "rich-tasting laksa." The word "laksa" itself means rice vermicelli, fine rice noodles. However, I know many chefs in Australia, London, and elsewhere who are familiar with this noodle soup, but make it with egg noodles, udon, or even soba noodles. Maybe they think their western customers prefer these to vermicelli; maybe the customers themselves think this. Well, all these kinds of noodle are suitable for laksa, although my preference is for the finer types. What matters most is to recognize and be able to make coconut milk of the right consistency. I shall say more about this in the introductions to some of my laksa recipes.

Laksa paste, like curry paste, can be made well in advance and stored in the refrigerator for up to seven days. It can be frozen in an ice-cube tray or small self-sealing plastic freezer bags. It's a good idea to label these clearly and indelibly, and to write the date on them—especially if you are storing a collection of pastes in your freezer. **Makes about 1¼ cups**

4 to 6 large red chilies, seeded and chopped
6 shallots, chopped
3 garlic cloves, chopped
6 candlenuts (page 140), or 10 blanched almonds, chopped
2 teaspoons chopped gingerroot
2 teaspoons chopped galangal (page 140)
2 tablespoons coriander seeds, coarsely crushed
½ teaspoon shrimp paste (page 141, optional)
1 teaspoon salt
3 tablespoons tamarind water
2 tablespoons peanut or vegetable oil

❶ Put all the ingredients in a blender or food processor and process for 1 minute. Add ¾ cup cold water and continue processing for 2 minutes longer.
❷ Transfer the smooth paste to a saucepan and cook at just above simmering point for 40 minutes.
❸ Leave the paste to cool completely and store as described above. Use as required, and in the quantities given in the recipes.

relishes and dry condiments

All of the condiments in this section have good strong
flavors of their own, but their real point is to provide
the crisp, crunchy texture that delights all Asians—
as it does anyone who enjoys good food.

Crisp-fried green cabbage leaves

This "seaweed" appears only twice in this book—as a garnish for Fried Noodles on Portobello Mushrooms (page 53) and in the Braised Duck on Seaweed and Rice Noodles (page 96). It can, however, be used with many recipes, and, indeed, with a multitude of dishes that are beyond the scope of a book about noodles. Make just as much as you need, because it doesn't keep—the shreds won't stay crisp for more than about 30 minutes. The same treatment can also be given to shredded celery root.

vegetable oil for deep-frying
2 or 3 cabbage leaves (the green outer leaves are best), finely shredded and patted dry

❶ Heat the oil in a wok or deep-fat fryer. Add the shredded cabbage and stir-fry for 2 minutes. Scoop out with a draining spoon and drain on paper towels. This first frying can be done well in advance; a second frying is needed to make the cabbage really crisp.

❷ When you are ready to serve, heat the oil again and fry the cabbage for 1 minute. Drain, and use immediately as a garnish. The shredded cabbage will become crisp as it cools.

Crisp-fried dried anchovies

Dried anchovies are another very popular Southeast Asian snack also used as a garnish. Many western cooks are unfamiliar with them, however, and don't know how to cook them. They must be fried until very crisp, and served and eaten before they have time to become the least bit soft or stale. In an airtight container, they should stay in peak condition for four days or longer. Do not refrigerate them! When buying the anchovies, look for ones without heads, which are sold in many Asian food stores labeled *ikan teri* (Indonesian) or *ikan bilis* (Malaysian). If you can buy only dried anchovies with the heads still on, cut them off and discard before frying. Makes about 12 ounces

1 pound dried anchovies
1 cup or more peanut oil or corn oil

❶ Heat the oil in a wok to 350°F. Add the anchovies and deep-fry in 2 batches for 3 minutes each batch, stirring often. Using a draining spoon, transfer them to a tray lined with paper towels.

❷ For real crispness, you need to fry the anchovies a second time for 1 to 2 minutes. Make sure they do not start to burn.

❸ Leave the anchovies to cool completely, then store them in airtight containers until needed.

Crisp-fried shallots or onions

These are a very popular garnish all over Southeast Asia. They are also widely available already fried from supermarkets and some delicatessens, usually packed in plastic tubs. For once, I can recommend the commercial product—they are as good as homemade and will save you time and trouble. **Makes about 4 ounces**

1 cup vegetable or peanut oil
3 cups thinly sliced shallots or onions

❶ Heat the oil in a wok. Add the shallots or onions and deep-fry in 2 batches, stirring often, for 6 to 8 minutes each, or until golden in color. Lift them out with a draining spoon and drain on paper towels. Leave them to cool completely.
❷ Store in an airtight jar (not in the refrigerator) for up to 24 hours until needed.

Crisp-fried noodles

The best noodles for crisp-fried garnish are rice vermicelli, fine egg noodles, or somen. They will all, however, only stay crisp for 30 minutes at most after frying. **Makes about 1 ounce**

2 ounces rice vermicelli, fine egg noodles, or somen
vegetable oil for deep-frying

❶ Soak the noodles in warm water for 3 to 5 minutes. Drain well, spread them on a tray and pat dry with paper towels.
❷ Heat the oil in a wok or a deep-fat fryer. Add the noodles and deep-fry, a few at a time, for 2 to 3 minutes, stirring them constantly. Scoop them out and drain on paper towels.
❸ Crumble the noodles and use as garnish immediately, before the food goes to table.

Garlic-flavored fried peanuts

Several recipes in this book require crushed peanuts as a garnish. The following method of frying peanuts is by far the best—not just for garnishes, but to eat as a snack with drinks and to make peanut sauce. You can now buy large peanuts with the reddish outer skins already removed. Use these, and fry a good big batch of them—they will keep fresh in an airtight jar for up to a month, if you can keep people from eating them for that long. **Makes 1 to 2 pounds**

1 to 2 pounds peanuts
1¾ quarts boiling water
4 garlic cloves, crushed
2 tablespoons sea salt
vegetable oil for deep-frying

❶ Put the peanuts in a heatproof bowl, pour enough boiling water into the bowl to cover the nuts, and stir in the crushed garlic and salt. Cover and leave the nuts to soak for 45 to 60 minutes.

❷ Strain the nuts and discard the soaking water. Spread the nuts on a tray and pat them dry with paper towels.

❸ Heat about 2½ cups oil in a wok or deep-fat fryer. Add the nuts in several batches and fry for 4 to 5 minutes each, stirring frequently. With a draining spoon or scoop, transfer the cooked peanuts to a tray lined with paper towels.

❹ Leave the peanuts to cool, then put them in airtight containers for storage. If you store them in glass, keep them in a dark place. Use as described above.

Oven-dried tomatoes

It's worth making your own oven-dried tomatoes if you can spare the time. If you are using tomatoes with thick, tough skins, then skin them first; otherwise, leave the skins on. Makes about 2 pounds

about 2 pounds tomatoes, peeled (optional, see above) and cut into halves or quarters if large
4 tablespoons chopped flat-leaf parsley
1 tablespoon chopped dill (optional)
1 tablespoon chopped oregano
2 to 4 garlic cloves, crushed
1 to 2 teaspoons sugar
1 to 2 teaspoons sea salt
½ teaspoon cayenne pepper or freshly ground black pepper
3 to 4 tablespoons olive oil

❶ Heat the oven to 250°F.
❷ In a bowl, mix together all the ingredients, except the tomatoes. Taste and adjust the seasoning.
❸ Place the tomato halves or quarters in a single layer in a large ovenproof dish or several dishes. Spoon the oil and herb mixture over them, cover loosely with foil, and bake for 1½ to 2 hours until softened and lightly charred.
❹ Let them cool completely and then store in airtight jars. Use as needed; the tomatoes will keep, in their jars in the refrigerator, for up to a week.

Cucumber relish

**This relish is very popular all over Southeast Asia, and each country has its own version. This is the basic relish, but you can make it into Thai cucumber relish by adding 1 tablespoon fish sauce (*nam pla*, page 140) and chopped cilantro leaves.
Serves 6 to 8**

1 cucumber, peeled and cut in half lengthwise
2 to 6 bird's-eye chilies, finely chopped
2 tablespoons white distilled vinegar
1 tablespoon sugar
1 tablespoon chopped scallions or chives

❶ Remove the seeds from the cucumber halves with a teaspoon, then slice the cucumber thinly into half-moon shapes.
❷ Mix these and all the other ingredients together in a non-metal bowl, and keep in a cool place for at least 10 minutes before use. The relish can be refrigerated for up to 48 hours before it becomes stale.

VEGETARIAN NOODLES

Noodles with roasted eggplant and tomatoes

Narrow ribbon noodles (page 10) or round rice sticks (page 10) are my first choices for this dish. The preliminary slow roasting of the eggplant and tomatoes is well worth the extra time in the oven— during which they need no attention whatsoever —as it makes them taste wonderful. The rest of the preparation and cooking take almost no time at all. The result is a vegetable dish that is full of flavor and character, and is good at lunch or dinner or even on a picnic, accompanied by a green salad.
Serves 4 as a light meal

1 eggplant, cut in half lengthways and then cut into slices about ¼ inch thick
8 red or plum tomatoes, skinned, quartered, and seeded
½ cup olive oil
2 garlic cloves, crushed
3 tablespoons chopped chives or scallions
1 tablespoon chopped oregano or basil
1 teaspoon sugar
1 teaspoon fine salt
8 ounces narrow ribbon noodles or round rice sticks, cooked as described on page 14
6 to 8 anchovies in oil, chopped
3 tablespoons chopped parsley
½ teaspoon freshly ground black pepper

❶ Heat the oven to 250°F. Arrange the sliced eggplant and quartered tomatoes in a large baking dish. Mix the oil, garlic, chopped chives or scallions, oregano or basil, sugar, and salt together in a bowl; pour this over the eggplant and tomatoes. Cover the dish with foil and put in the oven. Leave it, undisturbed, for 1½ to 2 hours. (This roasting can be done at any time; if you let the tomatoes and eggplant cool and store them in an airtight jar in the refrigerator, they will stay fresh for up to a week.)

❷ Reheat the noodles as described on page 16. Put the noodles into a large bowl and, while they are still hot, add the chopped anchovies and parsley. Season with pepper and mix well.

❸ If necessary, reheat the roasted eggplant and tomatoes in a skillet. Taste and add more salt if necessary.

❹ To serve, divide the noodles among four warm dinner plates. Top with the eggplant, tomatoes, and the oil they were cooked in. This dish can be eaten hot, warm, or at room temperature.

Fine egg noodles with scrambled tofu

As I write, Chinese fine egg noodles are still not readily obtainable in all supermarkets, but you can use angel-hair pasta instead if you like. Somen noodles are also equally suitable.

Serves 4 as a light lunch

1 block of fresh Chinese tofu or
2 blocks of firm Japanese tofu
1 pound young spinach leaves
8 to 12 ounces fine egg noodles,
cooked as described on page 14
4 tablespoons melted clarified butter (page 140)
or sunflower oil
4 scallions, thinly sliced
2 teaspoons finely chopped gingerroot

¼ teaspoon ground dried chili pepper
2 to 3 extra-large eggs, lightly beaten
1 tablespoon light soy sauce
salt and freshly ground black pepper
¼ teaspoon grated nutmeg
plenty of cilantro leaves, to garnish
soy sauce or Basic Chili Sauce (page 33),
to serve

❶ If using fresh Chinese tofu, rinse it well, then drain it and cut it into small dice; the firm Japanese tofu simply needs to be diced.

❷ Heat 3 tablespoons of the clarified butter or oil in a hot wok. Add the scallions, ginger, and ground chili and stir-fry for 2 minutes. Add the diced tofu and continue stir-frying for 2 minutes longer.

❸ Add the beaten egg and soy sauce. Stir and scramble the tofu with the eggs and season with salt and pepper. Turn off the heat and cover the wok.

❹ Heat the remaining clarified butter or oil in a saucepan. Add the spinach leaves with salt and the nutmeg, stir, cover the pan, and let the spinach cook for 2 minutes.

❺ Reheat the noodles as described on page 16 and divide them equally among four warm plates or bowls. Mix the spinach into the scrambled tofu and arrange on top of the noodles.

❻ Serve immediately, garnished with cilantro leaves and with soy sauce or the chili sauce in small bowls by each plate so people can add them as they wish.

Basic fried noodles

The possible accompaniments to fried noodles are endless—practically any broiled meat or fish, for a start. Char-siu pork (page 140), Peking duck (page 139), or any combination of stir-fried vegetables, are among my first choices. You can also try them with curry.

You can freeze these basic fried noodles for up to two months. Defrost them completely before you reheat them, tightly covered with foil, in a conventional oven heated to 350°F for 5 to 8 minutes. With a microwave oven, cover them with paper instead of foil and heat on full power for 3 minutes.

Serves 4 as part of a main course

2 to 3 tablespoons peanut or sunflower oil
4 shallots or 1 onion, thinly sliced
4 carrots, diced
8 cups quartered button mushrooms
2 garlic cloves, thinly sliced
1 teaspoon thinly sliced gingerroot
2 tablespoons light soy sauce
1 teaspoon ground coriander seeds
1 tablespoon tomato paste
salt
¾ teaspoon ground white pepper
8 to 12 ounces fresh or dried egg
noodles, cooked as described on page 14
4 tablespoons hot water or chicken stock
3 scallions, thinly sliced

1 Heat the oil in a hot wok or large nonstick saucepan. Add the shallots or onion and stir-fry for 1 minute. Add the carrots and mushrooms and continue stir-frying for 2 minutes longer.

2 Add all the remaining ingredients, except the noodles, hot water or stock, and scallions. Continue to stir-fry for 2 to 3 minutes longer to give the carrots time to cook.

3 Add the hot water or stock, turn up the heat, and add the noodles. Stir and toss all the ingredients over high heat until the noodles are hot. Add the scallions and stir again. Taste and adjust the seasoning.

4 Transfer everything to a warm bowl or serving platter and serve immediately.

Fried noodles on Portobello mushrooms

There are so many different ways of presenting fried noodles, even if you do not use meat. This simple vegetarian dish uses the big Portobello mushrooms as if they were edible plates, with the noodles piled high on top of them. The result is delicious, but you should eat this as soon as it's cooked. Try to time the operation so the noodles, mushrooms, and vegetables all finish cooking at the same time.

Serves 4 as a first course

4 large Portobello mushrooms, stems removed
2 teaspoons olive oil
salt and freshly ground black pepper
2 tablespoons peanut oil
3 shallots, thinly sliced
1 garlic clove, crushed
1 large red chili, seeded and sliced thinly on an angle
1 teaspoon chopped gingerroot
3 cabbage leaves, coarsely shredded
1 teaspoon paprika

1 tablespoon tomato paste
2 tablespoons light soy sauce
3 tablespoons hot water
2 carrots, cut into ribbon slices with a potato peeler
4 to 6 ounces dried egg noodles, cooked as described on page 14
handful of Crisp-Fried Green Cabbage Leaves (page 43)
handful of flat-leaf parsley or cilantro leaves, to garnish

❶ Heat the oven to 350°F. Brush the mushrooms with olive oil and sprinkle the open caps with salt and pepper. Arrange the mushrooms on the rack of a baking pan, and bake for 20 to 25 minutes: time this so the mushrooms are ready at about the same time as the noodles and the vegetable mixture.

❷ Heat the peanut oil in a hot wok or a large saucepan. Add the shallots, garlic, chili, and ginger and stir-fry for 2 minutes. Add the cabbage, paprika, and tomato paste and continue stir-frying for 2 minutes longer.

❸ Add the soy sauce and water, stir once, cover the wok or pan, lower the heat, and leave to simmer for 2 or 3 minutes.

❹ Uncover the wok or pan and add the carrots and noodles. Stir the whole mixture around, increasing the heat as you stir and scooping and stirring the noodles, for about 2 minutes so the noodles heat through. Taste and adjust the seasoning.

❺ To serve: put each mushroom on a warm dinner plate, gills upward. Divide the noodles and the vegetable mixture among the mushrooms, piling them high. Garnish with the crisp-fried cabbage and parsley or cilantro leaves. Serve immediately.

Timbale of fried noodles and spinach with green curry sauce

This simple, but very tasty, first course gives a new look to Asian fried noodles. The only special equipment you need are four 3½-inch ring molds. Serves 4 as a first course

6 to 8 tablespoons (or 3 to 4 frozen cubes) Green Curry Paste (page 40)
1 to 1½ pounds young spinach leaves
salt and freshly ground black pepper
2 tablespoons whole plain yogurt
1 teaspoon cornstarch, dissolved in 2 tablespoons cold water
8 ounces dried egg noodles, cooked as described on page 14
2 tablespoons corn or other vegetable oil

2 shallots, chopped
1 garlic clove, chopped
2 teaspoons finely chopped gingerroot
large pinch of cayenne pepper
1 tablespoon light soy sauce
1 tablespoon tomato paste
2 tablespoons Crisp-Fried Shallots (page 44), to garnish
handful of cilantro leaves or flat-leaf parsley, to garnish

❶ Heat half the curry paste in a pan. When hot, stir it with a wooden spoon. Add the spinach, cover, and cook for 1 minute. Add a little salt and, with a draining spoon, transfer the spinach to a strainer over a bowl and press the spinach down with the back of the spoon so the liquid that is forced out is caught in the bowl.

❷ Pour the liquid from the bowl back into the pan and add the remaining curry paste. In a bowl, whisk the yogurt with the cornstarch paste until smooth. Add this to the pan, stir the mixture, and turn off the heat. Adjust the seasoning with salt and pepper if necessary; set aside until ready to serve.

❸ Prepare to fry the noodles: heat the oil in a hot wok. Add the shallots and garlic and stir-fry for 2 minutes. Add the remaining ingredients except the noodles, and stir-fry for another minute; turn off the heat.

❹ Reheat the noodles as described on page 16. Heat the shallot mixture in the wok for 1 to 2 minutes. Add the reheated noodles and stir and toss them until the noodles and other ingredients are all well mixed. Taste and adjust the seasoning again if necessary.

❺ Just before serving, heat the curry sauce over low heat, stirring frequently, for 1 to 2 minutes.

❻ To serve, place a ring mold in the middle of each of four plates. Divide the noodles into four portions and put half a portion in each mold, pressing them down a little with the back of a spoon. Put equal portions of spinach on top of the noodles, followed by the remaining noodles on top of the spinach, once more pressing them down with the spoon. Lift off the molds and pour the curry sauce around the molded noodles and spinach. Garnish with crisp-fried shallots and cilantro leaves or flat-leaf parsley. Serve immediately.

Root vegetables with egg noodles

Serves 4 as a main course

main ingredients:
2 tablespoons extra-virgin olive oil
1½ cups thinly sliced red onions
1 cup carrots cut into julienne strips
2 large red chilies, seeded and thinly sliced
1 cup parsnips cut into julienne strips
1 cup celery root cut into julienne strips
4 tablespoons chopped flat-leaf parsley
1 cup cooked beet cut into julienne strips
½ teaspoon salt
12 to 16 ounces dried egg noodles,
cooked as described on page 14

for the yogurt sauce:
½ cup whole plain yogurt
1 teaspoon cornstarch, dissolved in
    2 tablespoons cold water
1 teaspoon sugar
½ teaspoon cayenne pepper
4 tablespoons hot water
salt and freshly ground black pepper

❶ Heat the oil in a hot wok or pan. Add the onions and stir-fry for 3 minutes. Add the carrots and continue stir-frying for 2 minutes. Add the chili, parsnip, and celery root, and stir-fry for 2 minutes longer. Lastly, add the parsley, beet, and salt and continue stir-frying for 2 minutes longer. Turn off the heat and cover the wok or pan.

❷ Make the sauce: in a bowl, beat the yogurt and cornstarch paste until smooth. Add the sugar, cayenne pepper, and hot water. Continue beating the mixture for 1 to 2 minutes.

❸ Transfer the yogurt mixture to a saucepan and season with salt and pepper. Cook, stirring all the time, over low heat until the yogurt is hot.

❹ To serve: reheat the noodles as described on page 16 and divide them among four ramekins, pressing them down a little with the back of a spoon. Unmold each batch of molded noodles in the middle of a plate. Arrange equal amounts of the vegetables around the noodles and spoon the yogurt sauce over the vegetables. Serve immediately.

Layered rice sticks with tofu, shiitake mushrooms and snow peas stir-fried with red curry sauce

Noodle bars everywhere are filled with loyal customers who love noodles, want fast food, and have been working their way through the menu for years. Those who, like Tampopo, have the time and inclination to experiment will often be rewarded. Here is an example of one direction you may find worth exploring—it's a vegetarian dish, but if you eat meat you can substitute slices of meat or fish for the tofu the next time you cook it. Serves 4 as a first course, or 2 to 3 as a light meal

main ingredients:
2 to 3 tablespoons peanut or sunflower oil
6 shallots, thinly sliced
2 tablespoons (or 1 frozen cube) Red Curry Paste (page 39)
3 cups sliced fresh shiitake mushrooms
4 to 6 ounces fried tofu, cut into 8 pieces
1 cup snow peas
3 scallions, cut on an angle into 4 pieces
8 ounces rice sticks, cooked as described on page 14

for the red curry sauce:
8 tablespoons (or 4 frozen cubes) Red Curry Paste (page 39)
4 tablespoons water or stock
½ teaspoon salt
1 teaspoon cornstarch, dissolved in 2 tablespoons cold water
½ cup whole plain yogurt
freshly ground black pepper

for the garnish:
Crisp-Fried Shallots (page 44, optional)
handful of cilantro leaves or flat-leaf parsley

1 First prepare the sauce because this will keep fresh for hours and can be reheated: put the curry paste in a saucepan, heat, and stir for 2 to 3 minutes. Add the water or stock and the salt. Bring to a boil and cook over medium heat, stirring often, for 3 minutes. In a bowl, whisk the cornstarch paste into the yogurt (this will prevent the yogurt from separating) and add to the pan. Continue to simmer for 5 minutes, stirring often. Adjust the seasoning and turn off the heat.

2 When you are ready to serve, start the stir-frying: heat the oil in a hot wok. Add the shallots and stir-fry for 5 minutes, until they are just changing color. Add the curry paste and stir well to mix. Add the mushrooms and stir again for 1 to 2 minutes. Add the tofu pieces to the mixture and keep turning them for 3 minutes. Add the snow peas, scallions, and more seasoning if necessary. Stir once, cover the wok, and continue cooking for 1 minute more. Turn off the heat and leave the wok covered.

3 Reheat the noodles as described on page 16.

4 To serve: put a small quantity of noodles in the middle of each plate (you can use a ring mold to guide you, if you like). Top this with a spoonful of the tofu mixture, then more noodles, followed by more tofu, and finally more noodles on top. Reheat the sauce and pour it around each pile of layered noodles. Garnish with crisp-fried shallots, if you are using them, and cilantro leaves or flat-leaf parsley. Serve immediately.

Caramelized shallots and eggplant wrapped in rice paper on spinach with oven-dried tomatoes

Oven-dried tomatoes are becoming so popular you can find them in most gourmet stores. However, if you make your own—and, better still, if you grow your own—they cost much less and taste better. The recipe for preparing them is on page 47.
Serves 4 as a first course

2 tablespoons extra-virgin olive oil
2 teaspoons sugar
12 shallots, halved
1½ teaspoons salt
3 tablespoons olive oil
1 onion, thinly sliced
2 eggplant, cut in half lengthways, each half sliced into 8 to 10 pieces
½ teaspoon ground dried chili pepper
2 tablespoons chopped parsley

½ cup chicken or vegetable stock or hot water
1 tablespoon clarified butter (page 140)
1½ to 2 pounds young spinach
freshly ground black pepper
large pinch of freshly grated nutmeg
8 rice paper circles (page 13)
4 to 6 ounces Oven-dried Tomatoes (page 47), to garnish

❶ Heat the 2 tablespoonsful of extra-virgin olive oil in a skillet. Add the sugar and stir until the sugar melts and lightly colors. Add the shallots and stir continuously for 4 minutes. Add ½ teaspoon salt, stir again, and turn off the heat.

❷ In another skillet, heat the 3 tablespoons olive oil. Add the onions and stir-fry for 5 minutes. Add the eggplant and continue stir-frying for 1 to 2 minutes longer. Add 1 teaspoon salt, the chili powder, parsley, and stock. Stir well, cover, and simmer for 20 minutes: check after about 10 minutes and add more stock or water if necessary.

❸ While the eggplant are cooking, melt the clarified butter in a saucepan. Add the spinach and cook, stirring it into the butter and adding salt, pepper, and nutmeg to taste. Cover the pan for 2 minutes; turn off the heat.

❹ When you are ready to serve, pour some hot water into a large bowl. One at a time, dip the rice paper circles into the water for 20 to 25 seconds each. Put each wet, and now pliable, rice paper on a tray and pat dry with a paper towel. Spread half a portion of eggplant on the rice paper, followed by some shallots. Roll up the rice paper, leaving both ends of the roll open. Repeat with the remaining rice-paper circles and filling.

❺ Divide the spinach among four warm plates. Lay two rice-paper rolls on each portion of spinach, garnish with blushed tomatoes, and serve immediately.

Vegetarian udon casserole

Choose five different vegetables from among those you like best. Prepare them, as described here, well in advance. The actual cooking time will be very short. If you are not vegetarian, use good chicken stock instead of water and serve this casserole as a vegetable side dish, to be eaten with a main course of meat, poultry, or fish. Serves 3 to 4 as a one-bowl vegetarian meal, or 4 to 6 as a vegetable side dish

main ingredients:
3 cups carrots peeled and cut into sticks
2 cups broccoli separated into flowerets
12 ounces bok choy cut in half lengthways
2 tablespoons peanut oil
1 teaspoon sesame oil
3 shallots, finely chopped
1⅔ cups thinly sliced fresh shiitake mushrooms with the stems removed
3 cups thinly sliced cremini mushrooms with the stems removed
freshly ground sea salt and black pepper
4½ cups coarsely shredded Chinese cabbage
12 ounces udon noodles, cooked as described on page 14

for the spiced broth:
2 tablespoons light soy sauce
2 teaspoons sugar
2 garlic cloves, crushed
½ teaspoon ground dried chili pepper
2 tablespoons finely chopped scallions
1 cup hot water
1 tablespoon sesame paste or tahina (page 142)

❶ In separate pans of boiling salted water, blanch the carrots, broccoli, and bok choy briefly; drain each and refresh in cold water.

❷ Make the spiced broth: mix all the ingredients in a saucepan and bring to a simmer, stirring constantly, until the sesame paste dissolves. Taste and adjust the seasoning with more soy sauce if necessary; set aside.

❸ Heat the oils in a Dutch oven. Add the shallots and stir-fry for 3 minutes. Add the mushrooms and continue stir-frying for 2 minutes longer. Season with salt and pepper, then turn off the heat.

❹ Now arrange the cooked vegetables in the Dutch oven. Imagine that the space in the pot is a cake, cut into five equal slices, but with a hole in the middle for the udon noodles. Push all the mushrooms toward one side of the casserole, so they become the first "slice," and away from the center. Arrange the carrots next to them, then the Chinese cabbage, then the broccoli. The bok choy goes on the other side of the mushrooms, so your "cake" is complete. Pile the udon in the central area.

❺ Slowly pour the broth all over the vegetables and the noodles, disturbing them as little as possible. Cover the Dutch oven and place it over medium heat for 4 to 5 minutes.

❻ Serve immediately, as hot as possible, and let everyone help themselves from the casserole.

Soba noodle soup with shiitake mushrooms and tofu

This is an excellent soup to start a vegetarian meal with or to serve before a main course of fish or meat. Guests who think they don't like tofu will love it when it is cooked this way; the sophisticated manner of its preparation and presentation will win them over before they even taste it. Serves 4

1 ounce white miso (see page 141)
2 teaspoons mirin (see page 141)
4 ounces firm tofu, cut into 4 slices
1 teaspoon salt
1 small eggplant, sliced lengthways into 4 thin slices
1 tablespoon all-purpose flour for dusting
peanut oil for deep-frying and sautéeing
1⅔ cups sliced fresh shiitake mushrooms

freshly ground black pepper
2½ cups Vegetable Stock (page 23)
1 tablespoon shoyu (see page 142)
1 teaspoon ginger juice (see page 140)
8 ounces soba noodles, cooked as described on page 14
2 tablespoons thinly sliced scallions

1 On a small plate and using a small spoon, mix the miso with 1 teaspoon of the mirin. Coat the slices of tofu with the softened miso; set aside.

2 In a bowl, dissolve the salt in 2½ cups cold water and soak the 4 slices of eggplant in this for 5 minutes to soften them. Remove the slices from the liquid and pat dry with paper towels.

3 Wrap each miso-coated slice of tofu in a slice of eggplant. Secure each roll with a wooden toothpick. Sprinkle the rolls with flour and deep-fry them in hot oil (350°F) for 3 minutes. Drain well on paper towels.

4 Sauté the shiitake mushrooms in a little peanut oil, stirring constantly, for 2 minutes. Season them with a little salt and pepper and drain on paper towels.

5 Heat the stock until it is almost boiling. Add the shoyu, the ginger juice, and the remaining teaspoon mirin. Taste and adjust the seasoning.

6 Reheat the soba noodles as described on page 16. Divide the noodles among four soup bowls, gathering and folding each portion in the bottom of the bowl so the noodles look neat and tidy.

7 Divide the shiitake mushrooms equally among the four bowls and pour the stock into the bowls. Discarding the wooden toothpicks, place a tofu and eggplant roll in the middle of each bowl and top with sliced scallions. Serve immediately, piping hot.

Avocado and tofu tempura in miso soup with soba

My youngest son, who loves avocado and tempura, commented that if I want this to be considered healthy food I should leave both of them out. Tofu and miso, he said, are good for you, of course, but not everyone likes them. I admit they may be acquired tastes, but most people who try them acquire the taste remarkably quickly. Tofu is rich in protein, and miso is said to reduce high blood pressure. So while you learn to love miso soup, its benefits will justify your enjoyment of tempura-fried tofu and avocado. **Serves 4 to 6**

main ingredients:
1 to 2 ripe avocados
vegetable oil for deep-frying
1 block fresh Chinese-style tofu, quartered, and each quarter quartered again (16 pieces in all)
8 to 12 ounces soba noodles, cooked as described on page 14
6 scallions, thinly sliced, to garnish

for the tempura batter:
2 egg yolks
2 cups ice-cold water
3¼ cups all-purpose flour
¼ teaspoon salt

for the miso soup:
2½ to 3¾ cups Basic Miso Stock (page 23)
1 tablespoon sake (see page 141)
2 teaspoons mirin (see page 141)
1 teaspoon light soy sauce
¼ teaspoon freshly ground black pepper

❶ First make the tempura batter in two bowls: put an egg in each bowl. Whisk the egg yolk in each bowl, adding half the ice-cold water to each bowl as you do so. Sift half the flour and salt into each bowl and stir lightly with a fork or a pair of chopsticks: don't beat the batter because it is supposed to be a bit lumpy.

❷ Peel the avocados, cut them into halves, and remove the pits. Cut each half across into 6 to 8 slices and put them at once into the batter in the first bowl: do not put the tofu into the batter at this stage!

❸ Heat the oil in a wok or deep-fat fryer. Add the batter-coated avocado slices, 4 to 6 slices at a time, and deep-fry for about 2 minutes, turning them over once. Remove and drain them well on paper towels. When you have finished with the avocado, start frying the tofu pieces, dipping them one by one into the batter in the second bowl and frying them as you did the avocado slices.

❹ When you are ready to serve, reheat the noodles as described on page 16. Divide them among four to six bowls.

❺ Make the soup: heat the miso stock in a saucepan and add all the remaining ingredients. When hot, pour the soup over the noodles in the bowls, and top with the avocado slices, then the tofu pieces. Garnish with scallions and serve immediately.

Coconut, tofu, and pumpkin noodles

This is a vegetarian version of a recipe given to me by my Canadian food-writer friend, Nathan Fong, of Vancouver. His original recipe is for a noodle soup with coconut, pumpkin, and shrimp, and he uses a chicken stock. You may prefer to follow him rather than me; but being fond of vegetarian dishes myself, I have chosen vegetable stock and tofu. Ribbon rice sticks are a good choice to go with for this soup. Serves 6 to 8 as a one-bowl meal

main ingredients:
3 to 5 tablespoons peanut oil
12 to 16 ounces Chinese-style fresh tofu, cut into 16 cubes
2 tablespoons Red Curry Paste (page 39)
3¼ cups Vegetable Stock (page 23)
1¼ cups thick coconut milk
3 cups peeled and cubed pumpkin
2 teaspoons chopped lemongrass (the soft inner part only)
2 kaffir lime leaves

4 scallions, thinly sliced
2 young celery stalks and leaves, roughly chopped
1 tablespoon Thai fish sauce (*nam pla*, page 140)
8 ounce rice sticks, cooked as described on page 14

for the garnish:
2 tablespoons Crisp-Fried Shallots (page 44)
½ to 1 teaspoon dried chili flakes (optional)
handful of cilantro leaves

❶ Heat the oil in a nonstick skillet. Add the tofu cubes in two batches and fry, turning them over after 2 minutes, then frying them for 2 minutes longer on the other side. Drain on paper towels; set aside.

❷ Heat the curry paste in a large saucepan, stirring continuously, for 3 minutes. Add the stock and coconut milk and bring the mixture to a boil. Add the pumpkin cubes and simmer over medium heat for 10 minutes or until the pumpkin is tender.

❸ Add the tofu and the remaining ingredients except the rice sticks and garnishes, and continue simmering for 5 minutes longer. Taste and adjust the seasoning if necessary by adding more fish sauce or salt.

❹ Reheat the rice sticks as described on page 16. Divide them among six or eight warm bowls. Pour equal amounts of soup, with tofu and pumpkin pieces, over the rice sticks in each bowl. Top with the garnishes and serve very hot.

Egg rolls

Egg rolls, in many different shapes and fillings, have been popular snacks throughout Asia for years, if not centuries. They originated in China, some time before the sixth century AD, when they consisted of crepes rolled and filled with the new season's spring vegetables, which is why you sometimes also find them called spring rolls. They were a welcome change from long winter months of preserved foods. Today's egg-roll wrappers are thin sheets of pastry, not crepes, and the range of fillings is enormous. This recipe is for cooked vegetables, but by all means add ground pork, chicken, or shrimp if you wish.
Makes 20 rolls

main ingredients:
20 frozen egg-roll wrappers, 8 to 10 inches square, defrosted
1 egg white, lightly beaten
vegetable oil for deep-frying

for the filling:
3 tablespoons peanut or sunflower oil
3 cups carrots cut into matchstick strips
1½ cups shredded white cabbage
7 ounces (drained weight) canned bamboo shoots, rinsed and cut into thin sticks
2 cups thinly sliced shiitake mushrooms, with stems removed
3¼ cups thinly sliced button mushrooms
2 teaspoons finely chopped gingerroot
3 tablespoons light soy sauce
3 ounces cellophane vermicelli, soaked in hot water for 5 minutes, drained, and cut into approximately 2-inch pieces with scissors
6 scallions, thinly sliced
1 egg white
pinch (or more) of ground dried chili pepper

❶ Make the filling: heat the oil in a wok or skillet. Add the carrots, cabbage, and bamboo shoots and stir-fry for 2 minutes. Add both kinds of mushroom, the ginger, and soy sauce and stir-fry for 3 minutes longer. Add the noodles and scallions and stir-fry over high heat for 2 minutes until the liquid evaporates, but the vegetables are still moist; season to taste. Remove the mixture from the pan and leave to cool.

❷ Place an egg-roll wrapper on a flat surface so one corner is pointing toward you. Put 2 tablespoons of the filling on this corner. Press the filling down a little and roll the corner of the wrapper over it, away from you and toward the center. Fold in the two corners that lie to your left and right. Brush the far corner of the wrapper with a little egg white and roll up the wrapper filling to make a neat cylindrical, well-sealed roll. Repeat with the remaining filling and the wrappers, making your egg rolls as even in weight and shape as possible.

❸ Heat the oil in a deep-fat fryer, wok, or pan to 350°F. Put four egg rolls into the oil, turn down the heat a little, and deep-fry for 6 to 8 minutes, turning them several times, until they are golden brown. Remove the egg rolls with a perforated spoon and drain on paper towels.

4 The egg rolls should be kept warm in a slow oven with the door ajar until you are ready to serve them all. Alternatively, let them cool, then refry them for a minute or so in hot oil just before serving.

5 Cooked egg rolls can be frozen for up to four weeks and reheated straight from the freezer. Heat the oil to 300°F and deep-fry the frozen rolls for 6 to 8 minutes so the filling is heated right through and the wrapper is crisp. If the oil is too hot, the wrapper will blister before the filling has defrosted and become warm.

NOODLES WITH SEAFOOD

Chopped shrimp and quail egg wonton soup with cellophane noodles

This delicious recipe will sharpen your appetite for the meal to follow. Serves 4 as a first course

8 large uncooked jumbo shrimp, shelled and deveined
2 shallots, finely chopped
1 teaspoon finely chopped gingerroot
4 teaspoons light soy sauce
large pinch of ground dried chili pepper
12 round or square wonton skins
1 egg white, lightly beaten
12 quail eggs
about 2½ cups beef or chicken stock

1 teaspoon mirin (see page 141)
1 tablespoon sake (page 141) or dry sherry
12 snow peas
salt and freshly ground black pepper
1½ to 2 ounces cellophane noodles, soaked in hot water for 5 minutes, refreshed under cold running water, then drained
finely chopped scallions, to garnish
cilantro leaves, to garnish

❶ Toss the shrimp with a large pinch of salt. Chop the shrimp with a large knife and mix them with the shallots, ginger, half the soy sauce, and the ground chili. (Alternatively, put these ingredients in a blender and blend them together for a few seconds.) Transfer to a bowl.

❷ Put one wonton skin on a flat plate or tray and brush around the edges with egg white. Place 1 teaspoon of the ground shrimp mixture in the center of the wonton. Make an indentation with your finger in the middle of the ground shrimp and break a quail egg into it. Gather the edges of the wonton skin together to shape into a bag or purse: the egg white will hold the edges together and seal the wonton just above the filling. Repeat this until you have twelve wonton ready to be put into the soup just before serving.

❸ Heat the stock with the mirin, sake or sherry, and the remaining soy sauce and bring almost to boiling point. Adjust the seasoning and add the wonton. Continue simmering for 3 minutes, then add the snow peas and simmer for 1 minute longer.

❹ Divide the cellophane noodles among four large warm bowls. Put three wonton and three snow peas into each bowl, followed by the broth. Scatter the garnish on top and serve immediately, piping hot.

Asparagus tips in clear broth
with crab wontons

The clear broth used here is the asparagus cooking stock, although you can, of course, use chicken or fish stock just as well. The stock needs to be light, however, without too many different concentrated flavors. You want the taste of the crab to predominate in the finished dish. Serves 4 to 6 as a first course

main ingredients:
16 to 20 wonton skins
1 egg white, lightly beaten, to seal
thinly sliced scallion and red chili, to garnish
light soy sauce, to serve

for the broth:
1 pound asparagus
2 whole tomatoes
2 celery stalks, each cut into 4 pieces
salt and freshly ground black pepper

for the filling:
4 ounces boneless pork meat with a little fat
8 to 12 ounces white crabmeat
1 teaspoon finely chopped fresh gingerroot
1 tablespoon finely chopped scallions
1 tablespoon finely chopped celery leaf
1 egg
1 tablespoon light soy sauce

1 To make the broth: trim the asparagus tips off about 2½ inches from the top; set aside. Put the rest of the stalks, the tomatoes, and celery into a pan with 1½ quarts of water and bring to a boil. Cover the pan and simmer for 30 minutes, then break up the tomatoes and continue to simmer for 5 minutes longer. Strain this stock into another pan.

2 Meanwhile, make the filling: chop the pork meat and fat with a cleaver until fine. In a bowl, mix the pork and fat with the rest of the filling ingredients, except the egg and soy sauce. Knead the mixture for a few minutes, then add the egg, salt and pepper, and soy sauce to taste and mix in thoroughly.

3 Divide the filling into as many portions as you have wonton skins. Put one portion in the center of a wonton skin. Brush the edges of the skin with lightly beaten egg white, then fold the skin to make a triangle, pressing the edges gently to seal it. Fill the other skins in the same way. (This is not the traditional way to fold wonton, but is the easiest and quickest.) You should now have 16 to 20 filled triangles.

4 Heat 5 cups water in a saucepan and add 1 teaspoon salt. Bring to a rolling boil and drop in 8 to 10 filled wontons. Boil for 4 to 5 minutes, then transfer with a draining spoon to a strainer to drain. Cook the remaining wonton in the same way.

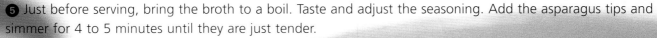

5 Just before serving, bring the broth to a boil. Taste and adjust the seasoning. Add the asparagus tips and simmer for 4 to 5 minutes until they are just tender.

6 Meanwhile, divide the wontons among four soup bowls and garnish them with scallions and chili slices. Pour the broth into the bowls and equally divide the asparagus tips between them. Serve piping hot. Instead of salt and pepper, let people help themselves to light soy sauce from a small pitcher or pourer.

Laksa lemak

This is the original laksa recipe, used to make the spicy noodle soup with coconut milk that was my own family favorite when I was a child in Java. We usually made it with rice vermicelli, slices of chicken breast, shrimp, and fried tofu.

Serves 8 as a first course, or 4 as a one-bowl meal

1¼ quarts Basic Chicken Stock (page 24)
8 tablespoons (or 4 frozen cubes) of
Paste for Laksa (page 41)
16 uncooked jumbo shrimp,
shelled and deveined
1¼ cups coconut milk
2 chicken breast halves (from making chicken
stock above, page 24), thinly sliced
salt and freshly ground black pepper

8 to 12 ounces rice vermicelli, rice
sticks, or egg noodles, cooked
as described on page 14
4 to 6 ounces fried tofu (see page 142),
thinly sliced
4 ounces bean sprouts
4 tablespoons thinly sliced scallions
handful of flat-leaf parsley
2 tablespoons Crisp-Fried Shallots (page 44)

❶ Heat the chicken stock in a large saucepan. Add the laksa paste and bring to a boil. Lower the heat and simmer for 5 minutes. Add the shrimp and simmer for 2 minutes. Using a draining spoon, remove the shrimp and set them aside in a bowl.

❷ Add the coconut milk to the stock and bring the soup almost back to boiling point. Lower the heat a little and let it simmer for 15 minutes, stirring often. Add the chicken slices, taste, and adjust the seasoning with salt and pepper if necessary. Let the soup simmer while you arrange the other ingredients in the serving bowls.

❸ Reheat the noodles as described on page 16. Divide the noodles among four or eight bowls. Place the shrimp and fried tofu slices on top of the noodles, followed by the bean sprouts and scallions. Pour the hot soup into the bowls, making sure the slices of chicken breast are evenly distributed.

❹ Garnish with parsley and crisp-fried shallots and serve immediately.

Laksa with udon, scallops, and quail eggs

Good fish stock, with beautifully cut carrots and a coconut milk soup of just the right consistency, makes this laksa irresistible. In the introduction to Paste for Laksa on page 41, I stress the importance of getting your coconut milk just right. I have often been served with laksa where the stock was delicious, but when I got to the bottom of the bowl I found the coconut milk cooling rapidly and almost solid. This shows that the coconut milk was not cooked at all. It is fine to use coconut milk from a can, but it must be heated so it is cooked even more before it is eaten. This is how to make coconut milk soup as it should be.

Serves 4 as a first-course soup, or 2 as a one-bowl meal

8 quail eggs
2½ cups Basic Fish Stock (page 21)
6 tablespoons (or 3 frozen cubes)
Paste for Laksa (page 41)
1½ cups coconut milk
2 carrots, peeled and cut into
thin flower petals
8 scallops with their corals
salt and freshly ground black pepper
8 ounces udon noodles, cooked
as described on page 14
handful of cilantro leaves, to garnish

❶ Put the quail eggs in a small pan of cold water, bring to a boil, and boil for 4 minutes. Drain and cool in cold water. Peel and cut in half.

❷ Heat the fish stock in a large saucepan. When it starts to boil, stir in the laksa paste and simmer for about 5 minutes. Add the coconut milk and simmer for 10 minutes longer, stirring often. Add the carrots and cook for 4 minutes. Add the scallops and continue to simmer for not more than 3 minutes. Taste and adjust the seasoning.

❸ Reheat the udon noodles as described on page 16. Divide the noodles among two or four warm bowls. Put the quail-egg halves on top and pour the laksa soup over the noodles, making sure each bowl gets an equal share of the scallops and carrots.

❹ Garnish with cilantro leaves and serve immediately.

Laksa with hot seafood pot

I recommend this particular laksa to anyone who lives where seafood is abundant
and can be bought really fresh. The best noodles to go with it are rice vermicelli,
which should be served and eaten in separate bowls, not mixed with the soup.
By all means use chopsticks to eat the noodles, shrimp, and fish, but drink the soup
from the bowl, Japanese-fashion (although this is not a Japanese dish). For me, this
is much more enjoyable than using a spoon; but if you really want to use a spoon,
of course, there's no reason at all why you shouldn't. **Serves 4 as a main course**

3¾ cups Basic Stock (page 23)
6 to 8 tablespoons Paste for Laksa (page 41)
1¼ cups coconut milk
salt and freshly ground black pepper
6 ounces monkfish tail fillet
4 ounces turbot fillet
12 large uncooked jumbo shrimp, shelled and deveined
4 ounces salmon fillet
4 ounces crabmeat (white meat only)

juice of 1 lime, about 2 tablespoons
handful of cilantro, or basil,
    or mint leaves, to garnish
2 red bird's-eye chilies, chopped,
    to garnish (optional)
12 ounces rice vermicelli, cooked as
    described on page 14

1 Heat the stock in a large saucepan. When it is hot, stir in the laksa paste and simmer for a few minutes. Add the coconut milk and continue simmering for 5 minutes, stirring frequently. Taste and adjust the seasoning.

2 Now add the monkfish fillet and let this simmer for 1 minute before adding (in this order) the turbot, shrimp, and salmon: the fish can be left whole or broken into portions if you prefer. Continue simmering for 2 minutes longer, then add the crabmeat, the lime juice, herbs, and chilies if using. Bring the soup almost to boiling point, cover the pan, and turn off the heat. Serve as soon as the noodles are ready.

3 Reheat the rice vermicelli as described on page 16. Place in a large bowl and moisten the noodles with a little of the soup from the seafood pot.

4 Give each guest a small bowl and let them help themselves to the noodles. Serve the soup and seafood in somewhat larger soup bowls, garnished with herbs. Eat the laksa and the noodles as described above.

Pan-fried scallops with endive and apples
on parsleyed soba or egg noodles

If you have freshly made soba or egg noodles, these are perfect for this dish, but dried noodles will do very well. Serves 4 as a first course

4 tablespoons clarified butter (page 140)
about 3 tablespoons extra-virgin olive oil
8 to 12 scallops, with or without corals
2 apples, peeled, cored, and each cut
into 8 wedges
16 endive leaves
large pinch of ground dried chili pepper
or cayenne pepper

2 tablespoons light soy sauce
1 tablespoon mirin (see page 141)
¼ teaspoon grated nutmeg
salt and freshly ground black pepper
6 to 8 ounces soba or egg noodles,
cooked as described on page 14
2 cups minced flat-leaf parsley

❶ In a large pan, melt half the clarified butter with the oil. When these are good and hot, fry the scallops, 4 at a time, for 2 minutes, turning them over twice during that time. Transfer them to a warm plate.
❷ Add the apple wedges to the pan and fry for 2 minutes on each side. Transfer these to a warm plate.
❸ Add a little more oil if necessary and fry the endive leaves until they wilt. Add the ground chili, soy sauce, mirin, and nutmeg. Return the scallops and apples to the pan and season with salt and pepper. Cover the pan, turn off the heat, and leave the pan, covered, for 1 minute.
❹ Reheat the noodles as described on page 16.
❺ Melt the remaining clarified butter in a wok. Add the chopped parsley and ¼ teaspoon salt and stir for 1 minute. Add the drained noodles and mix all together well.
❻ Divide the noodles among four warm plates and top them with equal portions of scallops, endive, and apples. Serve immediately.

Vietnamese stuffed squid with rice-stick noodles

This is a good party dish, hot or cold, with or without noodles; alternatively, you can take it on a picnic. The noodles make a contrast with the bright-red beet dipping sauce and the flavors go together very well. Soba noodles are also good with this squid. Serves 8 as a first course or a picnic lunch, or 4 as a main course

main ingredients:

8 small prepared squid, about 3 inches long, the tentacles reserved and chopped for the stuffing

8 to 12 ounces rice-stick noodles, cooked and drained as described on page 14

4 to 6 tablespoons Beet and Anchovy Dipping Sauce (page 27)

for the stuffing:

2 ounces cellophane vermicelli, soaked in hot water for 5 minutes, then drained

8 ounces lean ground pork

1⅔ cups thinly sliced fresh shiitake mushrooms with stems removed

4 scallions, thinly sliced

4 garlic cloves, chopped

1 teaspoon finely chopped gingerroot

1 large red chili, seeded and chopped

2 tablespoons chopped Vietnamese mint or spearmint

1 tablespoon Vietnamese fish sauce (*nuoc mam*, page 141)

large pinch of salt

1 egg, lightly beaten

vegetable oil for frying

❶ Prepare the stuffing: using scissors, cut the vermicelli into pieces about 2 inches long. Put these in a large bowl, add all the remaining ingredients, including the chopped squid tentacles, and mix well until thoroughly combined.

❷ To fill the squid: spoon one-eighth of the stuffing into each squid, pressing it down until the squid is about three-quarters full. Close the opening of the squid and secure with a wooden toothpick.

❸ Heat about ½ cup oil in a nonstick skillet. Add the squid and fry, turning them often, for 5 minutes. Using a needle or a fine skewer, pierce them in several places, then continue frying them, turning them often, for 5 to 6 minutes longer or until they are golden brown.

❹ Remove the squid from the pan and lay on a tray lined with paper towels to drain; remove the toothpicks. Leave the squid to cool a little, then, using a sharp knife, slice each one diagonally into three or four pieces.

❺ Reheat the noodles as described on page 16 and serve immediately, with the beet dipping sauce and the sliced squid.

Szechuan shrimp chow mein

I have been asked many times why I have never put a chow mein recipe in any of my books. Chow mein simply means "fried noodles," so evidently the time has come to produce this recipe, which otherwise I would simply have called "Szechuan shrimp fried noodles." **Serves 4 as a one-bowl meal**

24 uncooked jumbo shrimp, shelled,
cut in half lengthways and deveined
½ teaspoon salt
½ cup peanut oil for frying
4 shallots, finely chopped
2 teaspoons finely chopped gingerroot
1 teaspoon sugar
2 garlic cloves, very thinly sliced
4 scallions, thinly sliced
1 teaspoon Szechuan pepper (see page 142),
crushed in a mortar with a pestle until fine,
or 1 teaspoon ground dried chili pepper

1 tablespoon Chinese rice wine or dry sherry
1 tablespoon soy sauce
3 red tomatoes, skinned and chopped
½ teaspoon freshly ground black pepper
8 to 12 ounces egg noodles, cooked
   as described on page 14
2 tablespoons chopped cilantro leaves

1 Rub the halved shrimp with salt and keep them in the refrigerator while you prepare the spice mixture.
2 Heat 2 tablespoons peanut oil in a wok. Add the shallots and ginger and fry for 2 minutes. Add the sugar and garlic and stir-fry for 1 minute longer. Add the remaining ingredients, except the oil, noodles, shrimp, and cilantro leaves, and continue stir-frying for 2 minutes.
3 Heat the remaining oil in a skillet. When it is hot, add the shrimp and fry, stirring them all the time, for about 2 minutes. Remove them with a wire scoop and transfer to a tray lined with paper towels.
4 Reheat the noodles as described on page 16. Stir them into the contents of the wok and mix well. Add the fried shrimp and cilantro leaves and go on stir-frying for 1 minute longer. Serve immediately.

Singapore fried noodles

There are endless versions of this dish, which is also widely known in the west by its Chinese name, *char kwee teow.* **As a rule, the noodles are rice noodles—narrow or wide ribbons, rice sticks, or rice vermicelli. Whichever type you choose, I recommend you toss the noodles with the meat and shrimp mixture just before serving. Serves 4 as a one-bowl meal**

2 tablespoons peanut oil
3 shallots, chopped
2 garlic cloves, chopped
2 teaspoons finely chopped gingerroot
4 ounces lean, boneless pork, cut into julienne strips
1 red chili, seeded and chopped
2 tablespoons yellow bean sauce
1⅔ to 2½ cups sliced cremini mushrooms
   or shiitake mushrooms
1 tablespoon light soy sauce

2 teaspoons tomato paste
8 to 12 uncooked shrimp,
   shelled, cut in half lengthways
   and deveined
8 to 12 ounces rice sticks, cooked
   as described on page 14
4 ounces crabmeat
4 to 6 scallions, sliced on an angle
handful of flat-leaf parsley
salt and freshly ground black pepper

❶ Heat the oil in a wok or a wide saucepan. Add the shallots, garlic, and ginger and stir-fry for 1 to 2 minutes. Add the pork and continue stir-frying for 3 minutes. Now add the chopped chili and yellow bean sauce and stir well to mix everything. Add the mushrooms, soy sauce, and tomato paste and continue stir-frying for 1 minute. Add the shrimp and go on stir-frying for 2 minutes longer.

❷ After adding the shrimp, reheat the noodles, and drain them well. Transfer them to a large bowl.

❸ Continue stir-frying the meat and shrimp mixture for 1 minute (3 minutes stir-frying in total). Add the crabmeat and scallions, stir once, taste, and adjust the seasoning.

❹ Transfer the meat and shrimp mixture to the bowl containing the noodles. Toss to combine everything together and garnish with the parsley. Serve immediately.

Burmese fish soup with rice-stick noodles

This is a good party dish that can very easily be cooked in double quantities and put on the buffet for guests to help themselves from a big steaming bowl. The accompaniments can be arranged on an adjacent large plate. For a one-bowl meal to serve, say, four people, give each person a bowl of soup and a plate of bits and pieces alongside.

The accompaniments can be prepared a little while in advance—they do not have to be hot when they come to table, but the soup must be. Banana flowers may sound exotic, but they can be bought in many Asian grocery stores; if you can't find one, use canned palm hearts, which are easy to find.

Serves 4 as a one-bowl meal

main ingredients:
1 tablespoon peanut oil
2 shallots, thinly sliced
2 garlic cloves, thinly sliced
1 red chili, seeded and thinly sliced
½ teaspoon finely chopped gingerroot
2-inch stem of lemongrass,
outer leaves discarded and the
soft inner part finely chopped
2 cups coconut milk
8 ounces monkfish tail, filleted
and cut into 4 pieces
8 ounces salmon fillet, cut into 4 pieces
2½ cups Basic Fish Stock (page 21)
salt and freshly ground black pepper

for the accompaniments:
1 banana flower, the 2 outer layers discarded,
or 8 ounces canned palm hearts
8 ounces rice-stick noodles
2 hard-boiled duck or hen eggs, peeled
and quartered, or 6 to 8 quail eggs,
peeled and halved
1 to 1½ tablespoons chopped flat-leaf parsley
Crisp-Fried Onions (page 44)
Basic Chili Sauce (page 33)

1 Prepare the accompaniments: if using a banana flower, boil it whole in lightly salted water for 6 to 8 minutes; drain it. Cut it into quarters, then slice these across fairly thickly. If using palm hearts, drain the liquid, rinse, and drain again, then slice them very thickly. Put the banana flower or palm hearts on one side of the serving dish or plate. The rice-stick noodles are simply heated as described on page 16 and put in the middle of the dish. The eggs, parsley, and onions also go on the dish, and the chili sauce is served in its own bowl or bowls.
2 To make the soup, heat the oil in a large saucepan. Add all the solid ingredients except the fish, and stir-fry for 2 minutes. Add the coconut milk and bring to a boil. Add the monkfish and salmon and simmer for 2 minutes. Add the fish stock. Continue heating through for 1 or 2 minutes longer. Adjust the seasoning and serve immediately.

Caramelized cod fillet on rice vermicelli with yard-long beans in spicy coconut dressing

This caramelized fish is Thai in origin, but the yard-long beans in their coconut dressing take me back to my childhood—even at six years old I liked hot chilies. Thailand and Indonesia share a fondness for rice noodles. Of course, if there were not any noodles in the kitchen cupboard, we were perfectly happy to eat our fish and beans with plain boiled rice. Serves 4 as a one-bowl meal

4 cod fillets, each weighing 5 to 6 ounces
1 tablespoon lime juice
½ teaspoon salt
3 cups yard-long beans cut into 2-inch pieces
¼ quantity of Spicy Coconut Dressing (page 37)
3 to 4 tablespoons demerara sugar

8 ounces rice vermicelli, soaked in hot water as described on page 14
2 ounces Crisp-Fried Dried Anchovies (page 43, optional), to garnish

1 Rub the cod fillets all over with lime juice and salt; leave in a cool place while you do the rest of the preparation.

2 Boil the beans in slightly salted water for 4 minutes, then drain and refresh in cold water; drain again.

3 In the rinsed-out saucepan, mix the beans with the coconut dressing. Heat slowly, stirring them around with a wooden spoon for 1 to 2 minutes until they are just warm.

4 Spread the demerara sugar on a plate and coat the cod fillets all over with the sugar.

5 Heat the broiler while you reheat the noodles as described on page 16.

6 Broil the fish for 2 to 3 minutes on one side, turn them over, and broil the other sides for 3 minutes longer.

7 Divide the noodles among four plates. Put a piece of fish on top of each helping and spread a portion of beans and coconut around it. If you are using the anchovies, sprinkle them over all. Serve warm.

Tea-smoked monkfish with rice sticks and rujak sauce

I find this dish really great fun to make and I am always very pleased with the result. However, it does take a little time. The way to tackle it is to do most of the preparation well in advance, a day ahead if you can; then, on the day itself, you can bring this noodle dish to table in less than 10 minutes. Serves 4 as a main course

1¼ pounds monkfish tail fillet, in 2 pieces
1 tablespoon fine sea salt
scant 1 cup all-purpose flour
generous ½ cup light brown sugar
3 tablespoons black tea leaves
(Assam, Darjeeling, or Oolong)
12 ounces to 1 pound rice sticks (the narrow-ribbon kind), cooked as described on page 14

2 quantities Rujak Sauce (page 30)
1 green apple, peeled, cored, and diced
1 small, not-quite-ripe mango, peeled and diced
2 cups watercress, trimmed

❶ Well ahead, ideally the day before, prepare the monkfish for smoking: rub the fish fillet all over with the salt and leave in the refrigerator for at least 2 hours, or overnight. Rinse off the salt under cold running water and dry well by patting with paper towels.

❷ Use a double thickness of aluminum foil to line a thick-bottomed saucepan with a tight-fitting lid or a wok with a domed lid. Spread the flour, sugar, and tea on the foil. Place a wire rack over these and lay the fish on the rack. Cover the pan or wok tightly and put it over medium heat for 6 minutes. Turn the fish over and continue smoking for 6 minutes longer. Transfer the fish to a plate; set aside.

❸ When you are ready to serve, reheat the noodles as described on page 16. Drain them well and put them in a warm bowl; cover the bowl to keep the noodles warm.

4 Pour one quantity of the Rujak Sauce into a skillet and heat slowly. Cut each piece of fish in half (making 4 portions altogether) and place these side by side in the warm sauce. Leave them to simmer for 1 minute, then turn them over and continue simmering for another minute; turn off the heat and cover the pan.

5 Put a slice of fish in the middle of each of four warm plates. Arrange the apples, mangoes, and watercress on top of the fish, letting some fall to the side. Toss the noodles with the sauce from the pan and arrange them around the fish. Serve warm.

6 Serve the remaining rujak sauce in four small bowls as an extra dipping sauce.

NOODLES WITH POULTRY

Indonesian chicken soup with rice noodles

Chicken soup is as loved in Indonesia as everywhere else. Serves 6 to 8 as a first course, or 4 as a one-bowl meal

main ingredients:
1 small chicken, quartered
1 teaspoon salt

for the garnish:
8 ounces rice noodles, cooked
as described on page 14
4 ounces bean sprouts
1 tablespoon chopped flat-leaf parsley
1 tablespoon chopped scallion
4 or 8 lemon slices
2 tablespoons Crisp-Fried Shallots (page 44)

for the paste:
6 shallots or 1 large onion, chopped
3 garlic cloves, chopped
1-inch piece of gingerroot,
peeled and chopped
3 candlenuts (page 140) or 5 blanched
almonds, chopped
¼ teaspoon turmeric
½ teaspoon ground dried chili pepper
2 tablespoons peanut or olive oil
2 tablespoons hot water

1 Bring 1½ quarts water to a boil in a large pan. Add the chicken pieces and the salt and simmer for 50 minutes, skimming the surface as necessary.

2 Put all the ingredients for the paste in a blender and blend for a few seconds only. Transfer this rough paste to a bowl; set aside.

3 When the chicken is cooked, strain the stock and reserve. When the meat is cool enough to handle, shred it into small pieces, discarding the fat but keeping the bones.

4 Put the paste from the bowl into a clean saucepan and heat it, stirring all the time, for 3 minutes. Add the chicken bones and half the stock, cover the pan, and simmer for 15 minutes.

5 Strain the stock into another saucepan and add the remaining stock. Return to a boil and simmer for 15 minutes, skimming if necessary. Put in the chicken meat and simmer for 5 minutes longer.

6 To serve as a one-bowl meal: reheat the cooked rice noodles as described on page 16 and divide among four warm bowls. Divide the rest of the garnish (except the fried shallots) among the bowls and ladle the hot soup and chicken pieces over them. Sprinkle each bowl with the fried shallots and serve immediately.

Chicken dumpling soup with butternut squash and udon

The main ingredients of this dish are enhanced by a hot-and-sour broth, for which I find Paste for Laksa (page 41) particularly suitable. The thick coconut milk is optional; the soup is still very good without it. You can use any type of squash in season, preferably one with a good yellow color for contrast to the pale soup. Serves 6 to 8 as a first course, or 4 as a one-bowl meal

main ingredients:
2 tablespoons lemon juice
salt and freshly ground black pepper
1¼ quarts chicken stock
4 tablespoons Paste for Laksa (page 41)
4 to 8 tablespoons very thick coconut milk (optional)
1 to 2 tablespoons lime juice, or more
1 to 1½ cups peeled and diced butternut, Thai, or other yellow squash
4 to 8 ounces udon noodles, cooked as described on page 14
handful of cilantro leaves, to garnish

for the dumplings:
⅓ cup shelled pistachio nuts
2 skinless, boneless chicken breast halves, diced
¼ teaspoon salt
¼ teaspoon chili oil (page 140)
1 teaspoon ginger juice (page 140)
1 teaspoon light soy sauce
1 egg white, lightly beaten

❶ Prepare the dumplings: in a small pan of water, boil the pistachio nuts for 2 minutes; drain. When cool enough to handle, peel off the skins. Put the nuts and all the other dumpling ingredients, except the egg white, in a blender and blend for a few seconds. Transfer to a bowl, add the egg white, and stir with a fork or wooden spoon in one direction only for 2 minutes. Chill for 20 to 30 minutes.

❷ I like my dumplings small (so they can be easily picked up with chopsticks or in a soup spoon), so I divide the chicken paste into three portions and roll each portion on a sheet of foil to make a link-sausage shape about ½ inch in diameter, or a little thicker. Cut each sausage on an angle into dumplings about ¾ inch long.

❸ Bring about half a panful of water to a boil and add the lemon juice and some salt. Plunge a few dumplings into the boiling water and boil them for 6 to 8 minutes, then scoop them out with a draining spoon; set aside in a bowl. Repeat until all the dumplings are boiled.

❹ Heat the stock in a saucepan with the laksa paste and simmer for 3 minutes. Add the coconut milk, if using. Bring almost to a boil again, then add the squash and cook for 5 minutes until this is tender. Add the lime or lemon juice, taste and adjust the seasoning. Add the dumplings and continue cooking for 2 minutes longer.

❺ When ready to serve, reheat the noodles as described on page 16. Arrange the noodles in the bowls and ladle the soup, squash, and dumplings over the noodles. Serve piping hot, garnished with cilantro leaves.

Egg noodles with chicken and shiitake mushrooms

Fine egg noodles or angel-hair pasta are suitable for this recipe. It's a very practical dish, as everything can be prepared well in advance. You could very easily use the cooked chicken left over from making the chicken stock on page 24.

Serves 4 as a first course, or 2 as a one-bowl meal

main ingredients:

4 skinless, boneless chicken breast halves, sliced very thinly across the grain
2 tablespoons peanut or other vegetable oil
1⅔ cups sliced fresh shiitake mushrooms
1 teaspoon finely chopped gingerroot
4 scallions, thinly sliced on an angle
8 ounces fine egg noodles or angel-hair pasta, cooked as described on page 14
2 tablespoons light soy sauce
2 teaspoons sesame oil
1 teaspoon chopped garlic
salt and freshly ground black pepper
handful of cilantro leaves, to garnish

for the marinade:

1 tablespoon sake (see page 141) or dry sherry
1 teaspoon light soy sauce
1 teaspoon mirin (see page 141) or honey
¼ teaspoon cayenne pepper
2 teaspoons lemon juice

❶ Make the marinade by mixing all the ingredients in a glass bowl. Add the chicken slices and mix well. Leave the chicken to marinate in the refrigerator for 30 minutes to 1 hour.

❷ At the end of this time, drain the chicken. Heat the oil in a wok or skillet. Add the chicken and stir-fry for 4 minutes. Add the shiitake mushrooms and ginger and continue stir-frying for 2 to 3 minutes longer. Stir in the scallions, stir-fry for 1 minute, and remove from the heat.

❸ When you are ready to serve, reheat the noodles as described on page 16. Transfer them to a large warm serving bowl.

❹ Put the soy sauce, sesame oil, and chopped garlic into a small saucepan and heat slowly for 2 minutes. Pour the mixture over the noodles and toss to mix well. Season with salt and pepper.

❺ Reheat the chicken and shiitake briefly, then add these to the noodles and toss again to mix well. Adjust the seasoning and serve immediately, garnished with cilantro leaves.

Chicken wing party noodles

This is a great party dish for older children—say, seven or eight years old and older.
You can buy chicken wings almost anywhere, fresh or frozen, in large plastic bags.
I recommend buying them fresh, cooking them well in advance, and then freezing
them. On the day of the party, defrost them, reheat, and serve with plain-cooked
egg noodles. **Serves 6 to 8**

2¼ pounds chicken wings
3 tablespoons lemon juice
4 garlic cloves, crushed
1 teaspoon salt
3 tablespoons peanut oil
2 teaspoons chopped gingerroot
4 tablespoons chopped scallions
2 tablespoons dark soy sauce

2 tablespoons light soy sauce
1 teaspoon freshly ground black pepper
2 tablespoons ketchup
1 teaspoon sugar
1¼ quarts chicken stock or hot water
1 pound dried egg noodles, cooked
  as described on page 14

❶ Put the chicken wings in a large bowl and rub them well with the lemon juice, crushed garlic, and salt.
Leave them for at least 1 hour or preferably overnight in the refrigerator.

❷ When you are ready to cook the wings, heat the oil in a large, heavy-bottomed saucepan. When the oil is
hot, put in the chicken wings and stir them around with a wooden spoon for 3 to 4 minutes. Add the chopped
ginger and scallions, and continue stirring for 2 minutes longer.

❸ Add both types of soy sauce, the black pepper, ketchup, and sugar and stir again for a few seconds. Add the
chicken stock or hot water. Bring to a boil, lower the heat, cover the pan, and simmer for about 30 minutes.

❹ Uncover the pan, adjust the seasoning, and continue simmering over low heat, uncovered, for another
30 minutes, stirring the wings around from time to time. They are now ready, either to be served immediately,
or to cool completely and then be frozen.

❺ To serve: reheat the noodles as described on page 16. Arrange the noodles on a warm serving platter and
pour the hot chicken wings and their sauce over them. Ask your guests to help themselves. They can eat the
wings with their fingers and use forks or chopsticks for the noodles. Remember to put several empty bowls on
the table for the bones.

Casserole of noodles with hot-marinated fried chicken

Fried chicken is delicious and all children love it, but I find frying a chicken at the last moment is a hassle. This casserole can be cooked well in advance; it only needs to be reheated over medium heat for 7 or 8 minutes. **Serves 6 to 8 as a main course**

main ingredients:	for the marinade:
8 boned chicken thighs, each quartered	3 tablespoons peanut or sunflower oil
2 skinless, boneless chicken breast halves, each quartered	1 large red onion, finely chopped
3 tablespoons all-purpose flour	1 teaspoon finely chopped gingerroot
½ teaspoon salt	3 to 8 small dried or fresh red chilies, left whole
¼ teaspoon freshly ground pepper	4 to 6 scallions, cut into ½-inch pieces
vegetable oil for deep-frying	2 tablespoons dark soy sauce
12 ounces to 1 pound egg noodles, soba, or udon	2 tablespoons light soy sauce
4 scallions, very thinly sliced, to garnish	½ cup brown-rice vinegar or red-wine vinegar
	½ cup chicken stock or any other good stock
	1 tablespoon sugar, or more, if you like it sweet

1 Several hours ahead, or ideally the day before, prepare the marinade: heat the oil in a pan or wok. Add the onion and fry for 5 minutes over medium heat, stirring all the time. Add the ginger and chilies and stir for 1 minute longer. Add all the remaining marinade ingredients and stir for another minute. Taste and add a little salt and pepper, if necessary. Transfer to a large bowl and leave to cool.

2 Season the flour with salt and pepper. Coat the chicken pieces with the seasoned flour. Heat the oil for deep-frying in a wok or deep-fat fryer to 350°F. Add the chicken in two or three batches and fry for 6 to 8 minutes each time until nicely brown, moving them about in the hot oil from time to time with a wooden spoon or chopsticks. Scoop out the pieces as they are cooked and put straight into the cool marinade. Turn the chicken over a few times in the marinade, cover, and keep in a cool place for at least 4 hours, or overnight in the refrigerator.

3 About 30 minutes before you are ready to serve, take the chicken out of the refrigerator if it has been left there. While it is coming back to room temperature, cook the noodles as described on page 14.

4 Put the chicken and the marinade in a large Dutch oven over medium heat and cook for 5 minutes or until the liquid is just starting to boil. At this point, if you want your casserole to be a little more chili-hot, take out 2 or 3 of the whole chilies, crush them with the back of a spoon, and stir them back in.

5 Add the cooked noodles and stir well to mix them with the chicken. Cover and cook for 2 minutes longer.

6 Serve piping-hot, garnished with scallions. Let everybody help themselves from the Dutch oven, spooning the casserole into large individual bowls.

Chicken wontons with oven-dried tomatoes

For this recipe I suggest you use round wonton skins, not squares. The resulting wontons will look very much like ravioli, and if you make fresh pasta you can use your own ravioli pasta instead of wontons. Serves 4 as a first course

main ingredients:

24 round wonton skins

1 teaspoon peanut or olive oil

8 pieces of Oven-dried Tomato (page 46)

Parmesan cheese, extra-virgin olive oil or soy sauce, to serve

for the filling:

2 tablespoons peanut oil

1 tablespoon clarified butter

4 tablespoons chopped young leeks

2 garlic cloves, crushed

2 teaspoons finely chopped gingerroot

2 skinless, boneless chicken breast halves, grou

4 water chestnuts, finely chopped

large pinch of cayenne pepper

¼ teaspoon finely ground black pepper

½ teaspoon salt

1 teaspoon fish sauce (*nam pla*, page 140)

1 egg

1 First cook the filling: heat the oil and butter in a wok. Add the leeks and garlic and stir-fry for 1 to 2 minutes. Add the ground chicken meat and continue stir-frying for 3 minutes. Add the remaining ingredients, except the egg, and stir-fry for 2 minutes longer. Taste and adjust the seasoning. Transfer the filling to a bowl and let it cool completely. When cold, add the egg yolk and mix well; reserve the egg white for sealing the wontons.

2 To fill the wontons: arrange 6 wonton skins in two rows of three on a flat surface. Brush around the edge of each with the egg white. Put a portion of the filling on each of three wrappers, then lay the other wrappers on top to cover the filling. Press the edges well together to seal them. Fill the other wontons in the same way. Lay the stuffed wontons on a tray lined with baking parchment and cover them with a clean damp dish towel.

3 When you are ready to serve, boil about 2 quarts of water in a large saucepan. Add a pinch of salt and 1 teaspoon peanut or olive oil. When the water is at a rolling boil, add four stuffed wontons, one by one, and let them cook for 4 minutes. Take them out with a wire scoop and drain them on paper towels. Continue cooking the other wontons in the same way.

4 While the wontons cook, heat the oven-dried tomatoes in a small pan over low heat. Serve the wontons hot, three per person, on warm plates with the hot tomatoes. You can, if you like, grate Parmesan cheese over each serving, as if the wontons were ravioli; alternatively, drizzle them with extra-virgin olive oil or soy sauce.

Braised duck on seaweed and rice noodles

The "seaweed" used here is the crisp-fried green cabbage leaves on page 43, but there is no reason why you shouldn't make this dish with real sea-vegetable or sea-spinach, whenever this is readily available. **Serves 4 as a main course**

main ingredients:
4 boneless duck breast halves
2 quantities Crisp-Fried Green Cabbage Leaves (page 43) or about 2 ounces sea-vegetable or sea-spinach
2 tablespoons peanut oil
3¾ cups warm chicken stock
8 ounces rice vermicelli, cooked as described on page 14

for the marinade:
2 garlic cloves, crushed
2 teaspoons finely chopped gingerroot
1 bird's-eye chili, finely chopped
1 tablespoon dark soy sauce
1 tablespoon light soy sauce
2 tablespoons lime juice
1 star anise
1 tablespoon peanut oil

1 Mix all the ingredients for the marinade in a glass bowl. Slash the skin of each duck breast half down to the meat at an angle several times along its length, then add them to the marinade. Stir well and leave to marinate in the refrigerator for several hours or overnight; take them out of the refrigerator about 30 minutes before you want to cook.

2 Just before you are ready to serve, prepare the cabbage and keep it warm.

3 Heat the oil in a deep skillet. When it is very hot, add the duck breasts and sear them, skin-side first, turning them over after 2 minutes. Cook the other sides for 2 minutes, then add the marinade and simmer for 5 minutes. Now add the chicken stock, cover the pan, and cook for 15 minutes, turning the duck breasts over once after 7 or 8 minutes. Uncover the pan and add salt to taste. Continue cooking for 5 minutes longer; by this time, the sauce should be very thick.

4 Reheat the noodles as described on page 16. Divide them among four warm plates. Cut each duck breast at an angle into four or five slices. Arrange equal portions of cabbage on top of the noodles and the duck slices on top of the cabbage. Pour a portion of sauce around (not on) each mound of noodles and serve immediately.

Vietnamese noodle soup with steamed duck

You can make this with boneless duck breast halves or with the legs from a Peking duck (see page 139)—if using the latter, you do not need to marinate them first. Use chicken stock or vegetable stock, not duck stock, because it is too strong in flavor. **Serves 4 as a one-bowl meal**

main ingredients:
2 whole duck legs or 2 boneless
duck breast halves (see above)
1¼ cups peanut oil or corn oil
1¼ quarts chicken or vegetable stock
3 cups roughly chopped bok choy
or Chinese cabbage
4 young celery stalks with the
leaves, roughly chopped
2 tablespoons chopped scallions
8 ounces rice-stick noodles, cooked
as described on page 14
salt and freshly ground black pepper
handful of cilantro leaves, to garnish

for the marinade (duck breasts only):
2 tablespoons light soy sauce
1 tablespoon honey
½ teaspoon salt
1 tablespoon lemon juice

❶ If using duck breasts: mix all the ingredients for the marinade in a glass bowl. Add the duck breasts and marinade for at least 2 hours or in the refrigerator overnight. Drain the duck and discard the marinade.
❷ Put the duck legs or breasts on a plate and steam them for 20 minutes over boiling water in a large saucepan or steamer set over high heat. (If you use a saucepan, rest a wire trivet or some other stable heatproof object on the bottom to support the plate. Pour in enough water to provide 20 minutes' steaming, but not so much that it can get on the plate with the duck.) Take out the duck; let it cool.
❸ Fry the duck pieces in oil for 5 to 6 minutes until nicely brown; drain and set aside.
❹ Heat the stock in another large saucepan. When boiling, add all the remaining ingredients, except the noodles and cilantro leaves. Taste, adjust the seasoning, and simmer for 2 minutes.
❺ Meanwhile, slice the duck meat and discard the bones (if you are using duck legs).
❻ Divide the noodles among four bowls and put a portion of the sliced duck meat on top. When you are ready to serve, pour the soup into the bowls, sprinkle with cilantro leaves, and serve immediately.

Sam Leong's Shanghainese noodles

Sam Leong is the Chinese chef at the respected Jiang-Nan Chun restaurant in the Four Seasons Hotel, Singapore. This is a new recipe he has devised, based on a beanstarch sheet. These glassy sheets made from mung-bean flour are, he tells me, typical Shanghai products. If you can't get them, use a small amount of cooked glass vermicelli instead. Conpoy are dried scallops, available from specialist Chinese food stores. They are expensive, but you need only a small amount. Crisp-fried, conpoy are used as a garnish. If you can't get them, simply leave them out—there isn't any satisfactory substitute.

Serves 4 as a first course, or 2 as a one-dish light meal

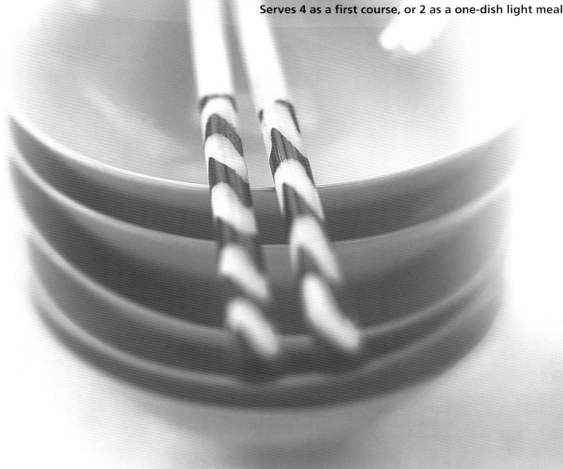

main ingredients:	for the sauce:
2 skinless, boneless duck breast halves, rubbed with salt and pepper, or 8 ounces roasted duck meat, such as Peking duck (page 139)	2 tablespoons peanut oil
	2 shallots, finely chopped
	2 garlic cloves, finely chopped
4 ounces green beanstarch sheet (see introduction), soaked in cold water for 1 hour to soften, then drained	1 red chili, seeded and finely chopped
	1 teaspoon finely chopped gingerroot
vegetable oil for deep-frying (optional)	2 tablespoons chopped celery leaves or flat-leaf parsley
12 fresh shiitake mushrooms, stems removed	2½ cups Basic Chicken Stock (page 24)
1 small celery heart, cut into julienne strips	2 tablespoons white rice vinegar
2 garlic cloves, thinly sliced	2 tablespoons Chinese red vinegar
2 ounces bean sprouts	1 tablespoon soy sauce
3 scallions, cut on an angle into ¾-inch pieces	1 teaspoon sesame oil
	a few drops of chili oil
at least 2 ounces conpoy (see headnote, optional), to garnish	salt
	2 tablespoons chopped scallions

1 If you are using uncooked duck halves, roast both breast halves in an oven heated to 400°F for 25 minutes. Leave them to rest for 2 to 3 minutes in a warm place, then slice the meat very thinly. Previously roasted duck only needs to be sliced or shredded.

2 If using conpoy, soak them in warm water for 45 to 60 minutes. Pat them dry, shred, and deep-fry until crisp.

3 Make the sauce: heat the oil in a wok or saucepan. Add the chopped shallots, garlic, chili, and ginger and fry for 2 minutes, stirring continuously. Stir in the celery leaves or parsley, then add the stock. Bring to a boil and simmer for 3 to 4 minutes. Add the rest of the ingredients for the sauce, except the scallions, and simmer for 3 to 4 minutes longer. Taste and add more soy sauce or salt, if necessary. Add the scallion and set aside.

4 Cut the softened beanstarch sheet into small rectangular shapes, about half the size of a standard sheet of lasagne. In a small saucepan, heat about ⅔ cup of the sauce. When it is almost boiling, add the beanstarch pieces to the sauce and heat for 1 to 2 minutes. Remove from the sauce, drain, and keep warm in a bowl.

5 Heat 4 tablespoons of the remaining sauce in a wok. When hot, add the shiitake mushrooms, celery heart, and sliced garlic and stir-fry for 1 to 2 minutes. Add the bean sprouts, scallion, and the cooked duck meat. Stir-fry for another minute, then add the remaining sauce. Bring to a boil and continue to cook for 2 to 3 minutes.

6 To serve: divide the beanstarch pieces among two or four bowls and divide the duck meat and sauce equally between them. Garnish with crisp-fried conpoy, if using it, and serve immediately.

Balinese ground duck satays on fried noodles

Fried noodles are a popular alternative to fried rice in Bali and elsewhere in Indonesia. They are usually served with at least one accompanying dish, often a satay such as this one. No sauce is needed here because the spice mixture is already in the ground duck. **Serves 4 to 6 as a main course**

main ingredients:
5 to 6 skinless, boneless duck halves, ground
ingredients for Basic Fried Noodles (page 51)

for the spice mixture:
2 shallots, chopped
2 garlic cloves, chopped
½ to 1 teaspoon ground dried chili pepper
1 teaspoon finely chopped fresh galangal or gingerroot
2 teaspoons cilantro seeds
1 teaspoon cumin seed
2 cloves
½ teaspoon ground cinnamon
½ teaspoon cardamom seeds
½ teaspoon freshly grated nutmeg
½ teaspoon turmeric
2 teaspoons chopped lemongrass, the inner part of the stems only
1 teaspoon sea salt
2 tablespoons tamarind water (page 142) or lemon juice
2 tablespoons peanut oil

❶ Put all the ingredients for the spice mixture in a blender and process to a smooth paste. Transfer to a saucepan and simmer, stirring occasionally, for 4 to 6 minutes; leave to cool completely.

❷ Heat the oven to 400°F. When the paste is cool, mix it well with the ground duck in a glass bowl. Knead the mixture with your hand for 1 to 2 minutes, then divide the mixture into twelve to sixteen portions. Form each portion into a ball, push a skewer through the middle of the ball, and shape the meat ball around the skewer to make a thick link-sausage shape. Repeat until you have used all the mixture.

❸ Meanwhile, make the fried noodles. Bake the satays for 15 to 18 minutes. Alternatively, heat a hot broiler and broil them for 10 to 12 minutes, turning them several times.

❹ Serve the satays as soon as they are cooked, either with the noodles or on the side in a separate bowl.

Quail stuffed with noodles and herbs

For this, buy quail that have already been boned or ask your butcher to bone them for you (try to get them still with the legs). The quail are to be stuffed with herbed noodles, then roasted. The result is deliciously crisp outside, tender and full of flavor within. Serves 4 as a first course or a light lunch served with extra noodles

main ingredients:
4 boned quail
2 tablespoons clarified butter (page 140), or olive oil
2 tablespoons chopped flat-leaf parsley
2 tablespoons chopped chives or scallions
2 teaspoons finely chopped garlic
1 tablespoon light soy sauce
4 ounces fine egg noodles, cooked
as described on page 14

for the marinade:
2 tablespoons honey
1 tablespoon lemon juice
1 tablespoon light soy sauce

❶ Mix the marinade ingredients together in a glass bowl. Add the quail and rub the mixture well into the skins; leave to marinate for at least 2 hours.

❷ Melt the clarified butter or heat the olive oil in a skillet. Add the chopped parsley, chives or scallions, and garlic and sauté for 2 minutes. Add 1 tablespoon soy sauce, then toss the noodles in the herb mixture. Take the pan off the heat and leave the noodles to cool.

❸ Heat the oven to 425°F. While it is heating, stuff the quail with the cool noodles, cramming as much as you can into the body cavity of each. Then make each stuffed quail into a little package, held together by string, or sew them up. Don't worry if a few noodles are left hanging out of each package; the final cooking will make them nicely crisp.

❹ Sear the quails in a little oil in a skillet, turning them around until they are brown all over. Place the quail on a roasting rack and roast them for 10 to 12 minutes. Drain them well with paper towels and leave them to rest for 3 or 4 minutes before serving.

❺ To serve: put each stuffed quail on a warm dinner plate and cut and remove the strings. With a sharp knife, cut each quail lengthways in half and arrange the two halves to show off the herbed noodles. For a one-dish light lunch, add more cooked noodles.

NOODLES WITH MEAT

Noodle soup with beef and lemongrass

This Vietnamese dish is equally good with or without chilies.
Serves 4 as a one-bowl lunch

main ingredients:
2 tablespoons vegetable oil
1 tablespoon tomato paste
1 teaspoon chili sauce (optional)
1 teaspoon shrimp paste (page 141)
2 shallots, thinly sliced
8 ounces narrow-ribbon rice sticks,
cooked as described on page 14
1 tablespoon fish sauce (ideally
nuoc mam, page 140)
salt and freshly ground black pepper

1 tablespoon chopped cilantro leaves
1 tablespoon thinly sliced scallions
½ cucumber, peeled, halved lengthways,
seeded, and sliced
2 romaine lettuce leaves, shredded
for the stock:
2 pork chops, some of the fat trimmed off
8 ounces chuck steak or brisket, in
2 pieces, some of the fat discarded
1 lemongrass stalk, cut into 3 pieces
½ teaspoon salt

❶ Put all the ingredients for the stock in a large saucepan with 2 quarts cold water. Bring to a boil and simmer for 60 to 70 minutes, skimming off the froth frequently. Take the meat out and leave to cool completely; strain the stock into a large bowl.

❷ Slice the pork chops and beef thinly, discarding the bones from the chops; set aside the slices of meat.

❸ In a small bowl, mix the oil, tomato paste, chili sauce, if using it, and the shrimp paste. Transfer the mixture to a large saucepan over medium heat, and sauté the paste for 2 minutes. Add the sliced shallots and stir for a few seconds. Add a ladleful of stock and simmer for 3 minutes. Now add the remaining stock and continue to simmer for 20 minutes.

❹ When you are ready to serve the soup, reheat the noodles as described on page 16. Heat the stock and add the fish sauce. Taste and adjust the seasoning with salt and pepper, if necessary.

❺ To serve: divide the noodles among four large individual bowls and put equal amounts of the sliced beef and pork on top of the noodles. Sprinkle the cilantro leaves and scallions on top of the meat, then ladle the stock into each bowl. Just before taking the soup to table, float the slices of cucumber and the shredded lettuce on top of each bowl. Serve immediately and eat while hot. An alternative way to serve is to put all the soup in a large tureen and let everyone help themselves.

Udon soup with sautéed beef and bamboo shoots

This makes an excellent one-bowl lunch or supper on a cold day. The secret of its fine flavor is to use a really good beef stock. Thinly sliced raw beef is available in Japanese food stores and some supermarkets. Serves 4 as a one-bowl meal

main ingredients:

2 tablespoons clarified butter (page 140)
12 ounces thinly sliced raw beef
2 ounces dried shiitake mushrooms, soaked in hot water for 10 minutes, then drained and sliced; or 1⅔ cups sliced fresh shiitake mushrooms
1 cup drained, rinsed, and thinly sliced canned bamboo shoots
1 tablespoon light soy sauce
12 to 16 ounces udon noodles, cooked as described on page 14
4 scallions, thinly sliced

for the broth:

1¼ quarts beef stock
1 tablespoon sake (see page 141)
1 tablespoon mirin (see page 141)
1 tablespoon light soy sauce
1 teaspoon ginger juice (page 140)
salt and freshly ground black pepper

❶ Put all the ingredients for the broth, except the salt and pepper, into a saucepan. Bring to a boil and simmer gently for 10 minutes. Adjust the seasoning with salt and pepper, if necessary.

❷ Melt the clarified butter in a nonstick skillet. Add the beef and sauté for 2 minutes. Add the mushrooms and bamboo shoots and stir them around. Stir in the soy sauce and about 2 tablespoons of the broth. Cover the pan and simmer for 2 to 3 minutes.

❸ When ready to serve, reheat the broth and the udon as described on page 16, until it is just about to boil.

❹ To serve: divide the udon among four large warm soup bowls. Pour the broth over the udon to cover them and arrange the beef slices, mushrooms, and bamboo shoots in equal portions on top of each bowl. Add the scallion on top or at one side of the bowl and top up the bowls with the remaining broth. Serve piping hot. Use chopsticks to eat the udon and other solids and drink the soup straight from the bowl. (You may, of course, use forks and spoons, if you prefer.)

Rack of lamb with asparagus noodles

For this I use the rack of single-rib chops. This is a perfect dish for entertaining because the chops and asparagus noodles can be prepared and part-cooked an hour or so in advance; the final cooking, just before serving, is done *en papillote*, with the lamb wrapped in baking parchment. **Serves 4**

12 to 16 lamb rib chops
½ teaspoon sea salt
1 tablespoon lemon juice
2 to 3 cups finely chopped parsley
16 garlic cloves
12 to 16 ounces very fine or wild asparagus

4 tablespoons clarified butter (page 140)
  or olive oil
2 teaspoons whole fresh green peppercorns
freshly ground black pepper
8 to 12 ounces soba noodles, cooked
  as described on page 14

❶ Put the chops in a bowl and rub them with the sea salt, lemon juice, and chopped parsley; set aside until you are ready to cook. Peel the garlic cloves and simmer them in a small pan of water for 15 minutes, then drain. At the same time, blanch the asparagus in a pan of lightly salted boiling water for 2 minutes; refresh in cold water and drain well.

❷ When you are ready to cook the lamb, heat the oven to 400°F and melt 2 tablespoons clarified butter or heat oil in a large skillet. Add the chops and fry in two batches, for 2 to 3 minutes on each side, turning them once. When the second batch have been fried, take the pan off the heat, put all the chops in it together, and cover the pan to keep them warm.

❸ Melt the remaining butter or heat the remaining oil in a wok. Add the softened garlic and the asparagus and stir-fry for 2 minutes. Add the green peppercorns and salt and pepper to taste. Finally, add the cooked soba noodles and stir them for 2 minutes so all the ingredients are mixed together.

❹ Cut four sheets of baking parchment to the size of a large dinner plate. Lay the four pieces of paper on a work surface and divide the chops and noodles equally among them, piling the ingredients on one half of the paper so you can fold the other half over them to seal; make sure each package has three or four garlic cloves.

❺ Seal each package by folding the paper over the chops and noodles and turning the edges as if you were making an apple turnover. Put the package on a baking tray and cook for 5 to 8 minutes. Leave to rest for 2 minutes.

❻ Serve by putting a package on each dinner plate and letting people open their own. They should use a knife and fork to slide the meat and noodles off the paper and discard the paper.

Black-peppered beef on wok-fried udon

Some supermarket meat counters sell beef steaks that are already crusted with black pepper, and you can use these if you prefer—but here's how to do it yourself from scratch. **Serves 4**

main ingredients:
2 tablespoons whole black peppercorns
1 tablespoon whole white peppercorns
about 1 teaspoon coarse kosher salt
4 sirloin steaks, about 6½ ounces each
1 tablespoon olive oil, if frying

for the noodles:
3 tablespoons peanut oil
2 shallots, finely chopped
2 garlic cloves, finely chopped
2 tablespoons oyster sauce or dark soy sauce
4 young celery stalks, with leaves, roughly chopped
3 to 4 ounces bean sprouts
1 teaspoon sugar
12 to 16 ounces udon noodles, cooked
    as described on page 14
4 scallions, thinly sliced, to garnish

❶ Grind the black and white peppercorns and the kosher salt together in a mortar, but not too finely. Spread the ground mixture on a flat plate and place the steaks on top, then press down hard to encrust the surfaces. Turn the steaks over and do the same on the other side; set aside the steaks until you are ready to cook.

❷ Heat the broiler to high and broil the steaks for about 5 minutes on each side, turning them once. Alternatively, heat the olive oil in a heavy-bottomed skillet. Add the encrusted steaks side by side and fry over medium-to-high heat, for 4 to 5 minutes on each side, turning them once; fry them for up to 2 or 3 minutes longer on each side, if you don't want them pink in the middle.

❸ While the steaks are cooking, prepare the noodles: heat the oil in a hot wok. Add the shallots and garlic and stir-fry these for 1 to 2 minutes. Add the oyster or soy sauce and celery and continue stir-frying for another 2 to 3 minutes. Add the bean sprouts, sugar, and a little salt to taste and stir for 1 minute longer; remove from heat.

❹ Reheat the udon noodles as described on page 16. Put the wok with the stir-fried ingredients over medium heat, add the noodles, and stir-fry for 2 minutes so all the ingredients are hot. Arrange on a warm serving platter.

❺ The steaks should now be almost ready to serve. When they are cooked, put them on a wooden chopping board and slice the meat thinly. Arrange the slices on top of the noodles and serve immediately, garnished with scallions.

Noodles with chili beef and fried basil

This dish comes from no country in particular, so you can use whatever noodles you choose or happen to have in the cupboard. My own choice would be either soba or fine egg noodles. **Serves 4 as a one-bowl meal**

main ingredients:
18 to 20 basil leaves
4 to 5 tablespoons vegetable oil
1 to 1½ pounds sirloin steak, cut into thin strips
2 tablespoons mirin (page 141) or dry sherry
12 to 16 ounces noodles (see above), cooked as described on page 14
light soy sauce, to serve

for the marinade:
2 to 3 large red chilies, seeded and chopped
4 garlic cloves, chopped
1 teaspoon chopped gingerroot
2 tablespoons Thai fish sauce (*nam pla*, page 141)
1 teaspoon sugar
2 tablespoons lime juice or lemon juice
2 tablespoons peanut oil
salt and freshly ground black pepper
2 tablespoons chopped basil

❶ Put all the ingredients for the marinade except the basil into a blender and blend until smooth. Transfer to a glass bowl and stir in the chopped basil. Add the beef and marinate for 1 to 2 hours.

❷ Heat the oil in a wok or skillet. Add the basil leaves and fry for 1 to 2 minutes, until they become translucent. Leave to cool completely; when cool, they will be crisp.

❸ Discard all the oil in the wok or pan except 2 to 3 tablespoons. Reheat the oil and add the beef with the marinade and stir-fry for 3 to 4 minutes over high heat. Splash the mirin into the pan and continue stir-frying for 1 minute longer. Adjust the seasoning with salt and pepper, if necessary. Turn off the heat and cover the pan.

❹ Reheat the noodles as described on page 16. Shake well and divide them among four warm plates or bowls. Top them with equal portions of the beef. Garnish with the fried basil leaves and serve at once. Instead of salt and pepper, put containers of light soy sauce on the table, so people can season their noodles for themselves.

Parsleyed egg noodles with lamb kofta in red curry sauce

Kofta is the Indian word for meatballs. These can be made with any meat you like, or even with vegetables; my *kofta* here are made of lamb and lentils. If you are a vegetarian, use lentils and fava or butter beans. **Serves 4 as a main course**

main ingredients:
1 or 2 egg whites, lightly beaten
4 tablespoons all-purpose flour
vegetable oil for frying
12 to 16 ounces egg noodles, cooked as described on page 14
2 tablespoons clarified butter (page 140)
2 to 3 cups chopped parsley
¼ teaspoon salt
Crisp-Fried Celery Root (page 43), to garnish (optional)

for the sauce:
6 to 8 tablespoons Red Curry Paste (page 39)
¾ to 1 cup coconut milk
salt and freshly ground black pepper

for the kofta:
⅔ cup red lentils
8 to 12 ounces lean ground lamb
3 shallots, finely chopped
2 garlic cloves, finely chopped
1 tablespoon chopped gingerroot
3 teaspoons ground coriander
½ teaspoon freshly grated nutmeg
2 tablespoons chopped mint, or
    1 tablespoon finely chopped fresh rosemary
½ teaspoon cayenne pepper
about 1 teaspoon salt
1 egg, lightly beaten

❶ Make the kofta: cook the lentils in boiling water for 5 minutes; drain. In a bowl, mix them with all the other kofta ingredients and knead the mixture for 1 to 2 minutes. Mold the mixture into meatballs, about the size of walnuts: you should end up with 20 to 30. Chill for 30 minutes to firm them before frying.

❷ When you are ready to fry the kofta (which can be done well ahead of serving), dip each one into egg white and roll in the flour. Heat the oil in a nonstick skillet or a wok. Add the koftas, six or eight at a time, turning them over several times until they are golden brown; drain on paper towels.

❸ Reheat the noodles as described on page 16. In a wok, melt the clarified butter, then add the chopped parsley and salt and stir for 1 minute. Add the drained noodles and stir all together.

❹ Make the sauce: cook the curry paste and coconut milk together in a saucepan for 6 to 8 minutes, letting this sauce bubble gently over medium heat and stirring often. Taste and adjust the seasoning. Just before serving, put the fried meatballs into the sauce for 1 to 2 minutes to reheat them.

❺ To serve, pile equal portions of the parsleyed noodles onto four plates. Pour the sauce and meatballs over the noodles and scatter the garnish, if using, over all. Alternatively, serve the noodles in one bowl and the meatballs and sauce in another, and let everyone help themselves.

Barbecued pork spareribs with shiitake noodles

You can eat this as a simple main course or as a one-dish meal. The spareribs can be prepared well in advance. Serves 6 to 8 as a one-dish meal or main course

main ingredients:

1 teaspoon salt

4½ pounds pork spareribs, cut into 3 to 3½ inch pieces

4 tablespoons oil

8 shallots, finely chopped

2 teaspoons finely chopped gingerroot

2 tablespoons dark soy sauce

3 tablespoons light soy sauce

2 tablespoons hoisin sauce

1 teaspoon sugar

1 to 2 teaspoons freshly ground black pepper

½ cup hot water

3 tablespoons Shaohsing wine (see page 141) or dry sherry

½ cup chicken stock

for the noodles:

12 to 16 ounces egg noodles, cooked as described on page 14

3 tablespoons peanut oil

1 large red onion, thinly sliced

2 teaspoons finely chopped gingerroot

2 garlic cloves, crushed

3¼ to 5 cups thinly sliced fresh shiitake mushrooms, stems removed

❶ Heat the oven to 325°F.

❷ Pour 3 quarts water into a large saucepan, bring to a boil, and add the salt. Stir to dissolve, add all the spareribs, and simmer for 5 minutes. Drain the ribs and pat them dry with paper towels.

❸ Heat the oil in a large Dutch oven. Add the ribs and stir them around for 4 minutes. Add the shallots and ginger and continue stirring for 3 minutes longer.

❹ Add the remaining ingredients, except the wine or sherry and the chicken stock, increase the heat, and cover the pot. Leave over medium heat for 3 minutes. Put the Dutch oven in the oven and cook for 1¼ to 1½ hours.

❺ Remove from the oven, turning the oven up to 400°F if you are going straight on to finish the dish. Add the Shaohsing wine or sherry and stir the ribs to coat them with the sauce.

❻ Remove the ribs from the sauce and arrange them side-by-side on a rack in a roasting pan. Transfer the sauce from the Dutch oven to a small saucepan. Up to this point, everything can be done well ahead of serving time—up to 6 hours in advance.

❼ Shortly before you are ready to serve, put the ribs in the hotter oven and roast for 10 to 15 minutes or until hot. Add the stock to the sauce in the saucepan and heat it slowly. Save 4 tablespoons of the sauce for the noodles and use the rest as a dipping sauce to be served with the ribs.

8 To prepare the noodles: reheat as described on page 16. Heat the oil in a wok. Add the onion, ginger, and garlic and stir-fry for 5 minutes. Add the shiitake mushrooms, stir for 2 minutes. Add the reserved sauce from the ribs and continue stir-frying for 2 to 3 minutes, then add the reheated noodles and stir-fry for 2 minutes longer.

9 Serve the noodles and ribs hot in separate bowls. The noodles and the ribs can be eaten together, or you may prefer to eat the ribs first, with the dipping sauce, and then the noodles as a course by themselves.

Pad Thai

Rice vermicelli, the Thais' favorite noodles, are the best choice for this classic dish, although I also use very fine egg noodles or angel-hair pasta. Serves 4 as a light lunch, accompanied by a green salad

main ingredients:
2 tablespoons peanut or sunflower oil
4 shallots, thinly sliced
2 garlic cloves, thinly sliced
1 teaspoon finely chopped gingerroot
8 ounces lean, boneless pork, thinly sliced across the grain and cut into julienne strips
2 tablespoons Thai fish sauce (*nam pla*, page 141) or light soy sauce
1¼ cups hot water
salt and freshly ground black pepper
8 to 12 ounces fine egg noodles, cooked as described on page 14
6 to 8 ounces watercress leaves
handful of cilantro leaves

for the garnish:
1 cup Garlic-Flavored Fried Peanuts (page 45)
2 ounces dried shrimp (see page 141), soaked in hot water for 10 minutes, then drained
1 teaspoon crushed chilies
pinch of salt

❶ First prepare the garnish: put the fried peanuts in a food processor and switch it on for 2 seconds only: the nuts should be only very roughly chopped; remove and set aside. Repeat this 2-second processing with the shrimp and chilies together. Put the processed shrimp and chilies into a nonstick skillet and dry-fry for 1 to 2 minutes, stirring all the time. Leave to cool, then put them in a jar and add the chopped peanuts with a little salt. Mix together with a spoon and put the lid on; this mixture will keep fresh for a few days if the jar is kept airtight.

❷ When you are ready to serve, cook the pork mixture: heat the oil in a wok or a large, shallow saucepan. Add the shallots, garlic, and ginger and stir continuously with a wok scoop or spoon for 2 minutes. Add the pork and continue to stir-fry for 2 minutes longer. Add the fish sauce or soy sauce and hot water, stir once, cover the pan and simmer for 4 to 5 minutes.

❸ Uncover the pan, increase the heat, and let the mixture bubble for 2 to 3 minutes, stirring occasionally. Taste and add salt, if necessary, and pepper. Stir again, until all the cooking juices are absorbed by the meat, but taking care that the mixture remains moist.

❹ While the pork is cooking, reheat the noodles as described on page 16. Loosen the noodles by hand and add them to the wok. Stir them around for 3 minutes and add the watercress and cilantro leaves. Stir again for a minute or so to get the noodles hotter.

❺ Put the noodles on a warmed serving platter, sprinkle with the garnish of peanuts, dried shrimp, and crushed chilies liberally, and serve immediately.

Rice-paper rolls with a fresh crunchy filling

I first tasted these in a Vietnamese restaurant in Paris, and I've watched people enjoying them in the Vietnamese market in Melbourne. They were delicious, with their hot dipping sauce. I recall that the filling contained bits of bacon, omelet, plenty of mint, and lettuce leaves. Here, I use mortadella rather than bacon and I don't cut up the omelet before I roll it inside the rice paper. Serves 4 as a first course

main ingredients:
8 rice paper circles (the largest size, page 13)
4 thin slices of mortadella, the hard edges trimmed off and each slice cut in half
4 romaine lettuce leaves
handful of arugula
handful of Vietnamese mint or spearmint
handful of cilantro leaves
2 small carrots, cut into tiny matchstick strips
2 quantities Nuoc Cham (page 31), divided among 4 small bowls, to serve

for the omelets:
2 tablespoons clarified butter (page 140)
6 large eggs, beaten
salt and freshly ground black pepper
1 teaspoon light soy sauce

1 First make the omelets: melt 1 tablespoon of the clarified butter in a nonstick skillet, tilting the pan so the butter covers the whole surface; pour off and reserve any excess. Season the beaten egg with salt and pepper and the soy sauce. Pour one-quarter of the egg into the pan and swirl it around to make a full round omelet. After 2 minutes, turn the omelet over and cook for 1 minute longer; transfer to a plate. Repeat this process to make four omelets in total. Cut each in half to make eight semicircles.

2 Pour hot water into a large bowl. Dip one rice paper circle into this and leave it submerged for 30 to 45 seconds. Lift it out, lay it on a tray, and pat it dry with paper towels.

3 To fill the rice paper roll: lay a semicircle of mortadella on the side furthest away from you. Fill the near side with a semicircle of omelet. Lay the lettuce leaves and arugula on this, followed by the mint, the cilantro leaves, and the tiny carrot matchstick strips. Start rolling the rice paper away from you into a neat cigar shape. Put it aside on an oval serving platter and repeat the process until you have eight filled rolls.

4 To serve: put two rolls on each of four plates and cut each roll across into four or six slices. Eat these with chopsticks, dipping each slice into your own bowl of nuoc cham.

Fried noodles with char-siu

Char-siu is the well-known Cantonese roast pork, available in the restaurants of any Chinatown. It is often displayed in the window, hanging from a hook next to the Peking duck. You can sometimes even buy it in large Asian supermarkets.
Serves 4 as a main course

12 to 16 ounces bought char-siu pork (see above)
Basic Fried Noodles (page 51)
Cucumber Relish (page 47), to serve
Soy Sauce with Chilies (page 31), to serve

1 Preheat the oven to 350°F.
2 Put the char-siu on a wire rack and heat it in the oven for 5–6 minutes.
3 Meanwhile, prepare the Basic Fried Noodles. Cut the thoroughly heated-through char-siu into thick slices and lay these on top of the noodles.
4 Serve hot, with Cucumber Relish on the side and Soy Sauce with Chili as a dipping sauce.

Mortadella on roasted peppers with rice sticks and asparagus in piquant thai dressing

It is probably easier to roast your peppers a day in advance, and make sure you save the juice from the peppers so you can add it to the dressing. Allow one big round slice of mortadella per person. Serves 4 as a first course

4 bell peppers (2 red and 2 yellow)
2 quantities Piquant Thai Dressing (page 35), plus the juice from the peppers (see above)
16 asparagus tips
salt

8 ounces rice sticks (the narrow-ribbon kind), cooked as described on page 14
4 slices of mortadella, the hard edges trimmed off and each slice cut in half

❶ Well ahead, ideally the day before, heat the oven to 325°F. Brush the peppers all over with olive oil, then roast them, still whole, for 30 minutes. Let them cool, then peel off their skins. Do this over a strainer, supported above a bowl, so that all the juice from the peppers collects in the bowl. With a spoon, take out and discard the seeds from the peppers. Cut each pepper in half.

❷ Shortly before you want to serve, put some of the piquant dressing in a bowl. Cook the asparagus tips in lightly salted boiling water for 4 minutes. Drain, and put it in the piquant dressing.

❸ When you are ready to serve, reheat the noodles, and drain them well. Put them in a bowl and toss with one quantity of the piquant sauce.

❹ Divide the dressed noodles among four warm plates, piling each portion on one side of the plate. Put half a red bell pepper on the other side of each plate, then half a yellow pepper slightly overlapping the red. Roll a half-slice of mortadella and place it on each pepper half. Arrange two asparagus tips likewise on each pepper half. Pour the remaining dressing over these and serve at room temperature.

NOODLE SALADS

Cellophane noodle salad with dried-fried shrimp, jicama, and apple in rujak sauce

The English name for Mexican jicama, yam bean, suggests the plant resembles any other kind of bean plant. It has pretty flowers, but they are toxic to humans and animals. The "yam" is the tuber that grows in the soil. A native of tropical America, jicama is nowadays widely cultivated in India, China, Indonesia, and East Africa. Easily found in any Chinatown, is it fruit or vegetable? For me it is a fruit; at least, I use it as one when I make rujak, a popular Indonesian hot-and-sweet fruit salad, but you can also treat it as a vegetable, eating it either raw or cooked. This combination of jicama, apples, noodles, and shrimp in a sweet, hot sauce is exotic and exciting, something not to be missed.
Serves 4 as a first course

1 jicama, peeled and diced
1 or 2 dessert apples, peeled and diced
1 quantity Rujak Sauce (page 30)
2 small red chilies, seeded and chopped
1 garlic clove, crushed
½ teaspoon salt
½ cup hot water
2 tablespoons chopped cilantro leaves
2 teaspoons grated palm sugar (page 141) or light brown sugar

2 teaspoons Thai fish sauce (nam pla, page 141)
24 to 32 peeled cooked jumbo shrimp
1 tablespoon lime juice
3½ ounces cellophane noodles, soaked in hot water for 5 minutes, drained, refreshed and drained again in a strainer, then cut into short pieces with scissors

1 As you prepare the jicama and apples, mix them into the rujak sauce so they do not discolor; set aside.
2 Put the chilies, garlic, salt, and hot water in a wok or saucepan. Bring to a boil and bubble for 2 minutes. Add the cilantro leaves, sugar, and fish sauce, and stir these around over medium heat until the sugar caramelizes. Add the shrimp, stir for 1 minute, add the lime juice, and turn off the heat.
3 Put the noodles in a large bowl, add the shrimp mixture, and toss together.
4 To serve: put a portion of the jicama and apples on the side of each of four plates, pile the noodles and shrimp on the other side, and distribute the sauce around the edge. Serve warm or cold.

Cold soba noodles with lobster meat salad

If you prefer, use narrow-ribbon rice noodles here instead of soba. Whichever you choose, however, the noodles need to be mixed with half the dressing while they are still hot from their first cooking. This helps keep them separate when they are cold, and of course the flavors of the dressing will have time to penetrate.

Serves 2 as a main course, or 4 as a first course

main ingredients:	for the dressing:
salt	3 tablespoons fish sauce
1 large whole uncooked or cooked lobster	2 tablespoons lime or lemon juice
8 to 12 ounces soba or rice-stick noodles	2 tablespoons hot water
cilantro leaves, to garnish	1 to 2 bird's-eye chilies, seeded
salad leaves, such as baby spinach, mizuna,	and chopped
arugula, and watercress, to dress (optional)	4 scallions, thinly sliced
	handful of cilantro leaves
	1 teaspoon brown sugar
	1 teaspoon finely chopped lemongrass
	(the inner part only)
	1 teaspoon peanut oil

1 In a large saucepan, bring 2 or 2½ quarts water to a boil with a large pinch of salt. When the water is boiling, plunge the whole lobster into it. Uncooked lobster needs to be boiled for 5 minutes; cooked lobster need be heated for only 1 to 2 minutes. Take the lobster out and set it aside to cool.

2 While the lobster is cooking, make the dressing by mixing all the ingredients together.

3 At the same time, cook the noodles as described on page 14, then immediately mix them in a bowl with half the dressing.

4 When the lobster is cool enough to handle, cut it in halves lengthways with a sharp knife and discard the inedible parts (the head sac, gills, and intestinal vein). Crush the claws and prise out the meat and chop the body meat into fairly large pieces. Put them all into a bowl and mix with the remaining dressing.

5 To serve: divide the noodles among the appropriate number of plates and top each plate with a portion of dressed lobster. Add more cilantro leaves to garnish, and some salad leaves, if you like. This noodle salad is to be eaten cold, but not chilled.

Cellophane noodle salad with shrimp and smoked salmon

Whenever I go to Thailand I look forward to eating the spicy fish salads that are so popular there, many of them mixed with cellophane noodles for the contrast in flavor, texture, and appearance. I love to make salads like this at home, too, but I know that if I serve them at a dinner party the dressing will have too much chili and fish sauce for some of my guests' tastes. This is a mild version, made entirely with ingredients that can be found anywhere, but by no means bland or lacking in bite.

Serves 8 as a good first course, or 4 as a light lunch

main ingredients:	for the dressing:
3½ ounces cellophane noodles	4 tablespoons lemon juice
16 very small button mushrooms	2 teaspoons sugar
salt and freshly ground black pepper	1 teaspoon salt
½ cucumber, cut in half lengthways and seeded	1 tablespoon light soy sauce
16 large cooked jumbo shrimp	1 bird's-eye chili, very finely chopped, or
4 ounces smoked salmon,	a large pinch of cayenne pepper
cut into julienne strips	1 small shallot, thinly sliced
16 Belgian endive leaves, to serve	1 tablespoon chopped scallions
	1 tablespoon chopped cilantro leaves

❶ Soak the cellophane noodles in hot water for 5 to 8 minutes. Drain and refresh under cold running water until cool, as described on page 14; leave the noodles to drain in a strainer.

❷ Boil the mushrooms in salted water for 2 minutes. Drain, refresh in cold water, and drain again.

❸ Slice the cucumber into half-moon shapes. Put these into a large glass bowl then add all the ingredients for the dressing, stirring to dissolve the sugar and salt: this dressing can be prepared up to 4 hours in advance.

❹ When you are ready to serve the salad, cut the noodles with scissors into 2- to 4-inch pieces so they are easy to eat. Stir the noodles, shrimp, mushrooms, and smoked salmon strips together and toss. Serve on top of the endive leaves.

Variation: With the same dressing and noodles, add two ripe avocados, each cut into eight slices. In place of endive, use eight romaine lettuce leaves and 7 ounces more smoked salmon, sliced, instead of shrimp and mushrooms. The avocado, salmon, and noodles on top of the lettuce leaves look particularly striking if you serve the dish on blue or yellow plates.

Nathan Fong's shrimp wonton salad

Once again, I have to thank my friend Nathan Fong in Vancouver for sharing his new recipe with me. There he uses what is called rock shrimp locally.

Serves 4 as a first course

main ingredients:
24 round wonton skins
1 egg, lightly beaten
handful of cilantro leaves, to garnish
handful of arugula leaves, to garnish

for the citrus-soy vinaigrette:
4 tablespoons extra-virgin olive oil
2 teaspoons sesame oil
1 shallot, finely chopped
2 tablespoons Japanese brown rice vinegar
1 tablespoon light soy sauce
finely grated zest and juice of 1 lime
finely grated zest and juice of 1 lemon
freshly ground black pepper

for the filling:
8 ounces uncooked shelled jumbo shrimp, deveined and finely chopped
2 scallions, thinly sliced
4 water chestnuts, finely chopped
2 tablespoons chopped cilantro leaves
1 tablespoon sesame oil
¼ teaspoon ground dried chili pepper or freshly ground black pepper
1 garlic clove, finely chopped
finely grated zest and juice of 1 lemon
salt

❶ Mix all the ingredients for the filling together in a glass bowl. Fry 1 teaspoon of it in a little oil and taste, then add more salt if necessary; set aside in a cool place for 30 minutes.

❷ On a flat surface, arrange two rows of wonton skins with three in each row. Brush around the edges with beaten egg. Divide the filling into twelve equal portions, and put one portion on each of the three wrappers nearest you. Use the wrappers from the next row to cover these, and pinch round the edges to seal well. Put these filled wonton ravioli on a tray lined with baking parchment, then fill the remaining wonton skins the same way, so you have twelve in total.

❸ Whisk together all the ingredients for the vinaigrette in a glass bowl; set aside.

❹ Bring a large pan of slightly salted water to a rolling boil. Add the filled wontons, six at a time, and boil for about 4 minutes each batch. When they are cooked, lift them out with a draining spoon and drain on paper towels.

❺ To serve: arrange three cooked wontons on each of four plates. Drizzle the vinaigrette all over them and garnish with cilantro and arugula leaves. Serve at room temperature.

Piquant salad of cellophane vermicelli wrapped in smoked salmon with cucumber and yogurt

For the best presentation of this dish, use ring molds about 3½ inches in diameter. Serves 4 as a first course or light lunch

1 ounce dried wood ear mushrooms
3½ ounces cellophane vermicelli, soaked in hot
water for 5 minutes, then refreshed under
cold running water, and drained well
1 quantity Piquant Thai Dressing (page 35)
4 inner celery stalks with the leaves, thickly sliced
5 tablespoons plain yogurt
salt and freshly ground black pepper
1 thin cucumber, peeled and thinly sliced
4 large slices of smoked salmon,
12 to 16 ounces total weight

❶ Soak the wood ears in hot water for 5 minutes, then drain and slice them thinly.
❷ For this cold salad, the cellophane vermicelli do not have to be reheated. Using scissors, chop the noodles into short strands, roughly 2 inches in length. Put these in a bowl and toss them with the Thai dressing. Add the celery and wood ears and mix everything together well.
❸ Whisk the yogurt in a bowl with salt and pepper to taste. Add the cucumber slices and stir so they are all well coated with the yogurt.
❹ When you are ready to serve, put a ring mold (see above) in the middle of each of four plates. Line each mold with a slice of salmon and pile the cellophane vermicelli, wood ears, and celery inside, pressing them down with the back of a spoon. Carefully lift the mold away from its contents so you do not disturb the salmon. Spoon the cucumber and yogurt around the salmon rings and serve immediately.

Vietnamese rice-paper rolls with herb salad

In my recent travels I've eaten these rice-paper rolls, in one form or another and with various fillings. They are sure of a welcome, provided they are freshly made and served immediately.

Makes 4 rolls (serves 4 people as a first course)

main ingredients:
1¼ quarts hot (not boiling) water
8 round sheets of rice paper, 11½ inches
in diameter (page 13)
8 young romaine lettuce leaves, coarsely shredded
1 ounce cooked rice vermicelli, cooked as
described on page 14
1 cup cooked honey-roast ham,
cut into julienne strips
16 peeled cooked jumbo shrimp
2 hard-boiled eggs, sliced
2 tablespoons roughly chopped mint
2 tablespoons roughly chopped cilantro leaves

for the dressing:
2 teaspoons Dijon mustard
juice of 2 limes
2 teaspoons chopped chives
1 tablespoon white-wine vinegar
1 teaspoon sugar (optional)
½ cup extra-virgin olive oil
salt and freshly ground black pepper

for the salad:
8 ounces arugula leaves
handful of cilantro leaves
handful of mint leaves

1 Make the dressing: in a glass bowl, mix the mustard with the lime juice. Add the chives, vinegar, and sugar, whisking with a fork. Add the olive oil, a little at a time, still whisking. Add the last of the olive oil in a continuous stream, whisking continually until the dressing becomes fairly thick. Season to taste with salt and pepper.

2 To fill the rolls: put the hot water into a bowl. Take two rice-paper circles and dip them into the water one at a time, leaving each immersed for 15 seconds to let it soften. Lay each circle on a flat surface, pat dry with paper towels. Lay the second circle on top of the first and pat dry again. Spread one-quarter of the shredded lettuce across this double-thickness, leaving about ½ inch clear around the edge. Sprinkle the lettuce with 1 teaspoon of the dressing. Next arrange one-quarter of the noodles on top of the lettuce, then add one-quarter of the ham, the shrimp, egg, mint, and cilantro. Finish with another teaspoon of the dressing over the whole pile. Fold the left and right sides of the rice-paper circles inward, then roll up the rice paper, starting from the edge nearest you, so all the filling is firmly rolled and held inside. Repeat to make four rolls in total.

3 When you are ready to serve, dress the salad ingredients with the remaining dressing. Divide the salad among four plates. Cut each roll into three slices and arrange these on top of the salad. Serve and eat immediately.

Green papaya and mango salad with cellophane noodles and marinated salmon and sea bass

This is a Southeast Asian raw fish salad—although not truly raw, as the juices of the papaya, mango, and lime (or lemon) actually "cook" the fish very slightly. Make sure you buy the freshest of fish. Serves 4 as a first course

1 small green papaya, peeled, seeded, and the flesh either grated or cut into tiny matchstick strips
1 tablespoon salt
1 slightly unripe mango, peeled and sliced into tiny matchstick strips
4 ounces cellophane noodles, soaked in hot water for 5 minutes, refreshed under cold running water, then drained and cut into short pieces with scissors
1 quantity Piquant Thai Dressing (page 35)

8 ounces skinless salmon fillet, cut into thin slices
8 ounces skinless sea bass fillet, cut into thin slices
juice of 2 limes or lemons
½ teaspoon fine kosher salt
4 romaine lettuce leaves, to serve
1 to 2 large red chilies, seeded and sliced, to garnish

1 Put the papaya flesh in a bowl and stir in the salt; leave for 30 minutes. Rinse the papaya in a strainer to remove the salt, drain again, and transfer to a large bowl.

2 Add the mango and noodles to the bowl and pour the dressing over; toss and mix well.

3 Put the slices of fish in another bowl. Add the lime or lemon juice and the fine kosher salt. Mix well and leave to stand for 2 to 4 minutes, then toss into the noodle mixture and leave to stand for 2 minutes longer.

4 To serve: put a lettuce leaf on each of four large plates. Divide the noodle salad equally among the lettuce leaves; if the leaves are not big enough to contain whole portions, let some fall onto the plates. Serve cold, garnished with slices of red chili.

Salad of cold somen with avocado dipping sauce and stuffed chicken rolls

My reason for having included in the first part of this book as many recipes for dipping sauces as space allows is that each sauce can be used with many different recipes. So do read those early pages as a guide to creating variations on recipes, and to adapting sauces to different uses—also to making basic sauces in large quantities for cold storage, so you always have them ready for use at short notice. Serves 4 as a lunch or supper, or 8 as a first course

main ingredients:
6 to 8 ounces somen noodles, cooked as
described on page 14
Spicy Avocado Dipping Sauce (page 30,
made with 2 avocados)
handful (or more) of watercress or arugula

for the stuffing:
salt and freshly ground black pepper
2 small carrots, diced
1 parsnip, diced
2 tablespoons clarified butter (page 140)
4 cremini mushrooms, stems removed
and caps finely diced
4 tablespoons chopped cilantro or parsley
1 tablespoon light soy sauce

for the chicken rolls:
3 to 4 skinless, boneless chicken breast halves,
about 1 pound total weight, diced
2 eggs, lightly beaten
1 teaspoon very finely chopped gingerroot
½ teaspoon salt
1 garlic clove, crushed
2 teaspoons cornstarch, dissolved in
2 tablespoons cold water
1 tablespoon light soy sauce
1 teaspoon sugar

❶ Put all ingredients for the chicken rolls in a blender or food processor and blend until smooth; transfer to a plate and keep in a cool place.

❷ Prepare the stuffing: in separate small pans of lightly salted boiling water, blanch the carrots and parsnips for 2 minutes and 1 minute respectively; drain, refresh in cold water, and drain well again.

❸ Melt the clarified butter in a nonstick skillet. Add the mushrooms and stir-fry for 2 minutes. Add the cilantro or parsley and stir for 1 minute. Stir in the carrots and parsnips and season with ½ teaspoon each salt and pepper, and the soy sauce. Stir-fry for just 1 minute longer. Turn off the heat and leave to cool.

❹ Divide the chicken mixture into three. Lay a piece of plastic wrap on a tray and put one portion of the ground chicken on the plastic wrap, molding and pressing it to form a square, as if you were making pastry.

Spread one-third of the stuffing in a strip across the middle of the square. Now pick up the edge of plastic nearest you and carefully roll up the stuffing inside the chicken to make a kind of thick link sausage: take care not to get the edge of the plastic wrap caught in the mixture. Twist the plastic wrap on both ends to seal and tie closed with string. Repeat this process to make two more rolls.

5 Lay the rolls on a plate that will fit into a steamer. Steam them for 10 to 15 minutes. Leave the rolls to cool a little, unwrap them from the plastic wrap, and cut each roll across into slices about ½ inch thick.

6 To serve: arrange the noodles on four or eight plates. Spoon equal portions of the dipping sauce over the noodles. Arrange the sliced chicken rolls around each mound of noodles and top with watercress or arugula. Or toss everything together in a bowl. Serve at room temperature.

Warm salad of duck, green beans, and roasted peppers with fried rice-stick noodles

As a rule, when I am cooking just for two I don't want to spend more than 20 minutes in the kitchen before I sit down to enjoy the food, and this is one of the recipes I make often. Remember, though, to roast the peppers well beforehand—on the previous day, even—because this takes 30 minutes.

Serves 2 as a one-bowl meal, or 4 as a first course

main ingredients:	for the fried noodles:
2 bell peppers (preferably 1 red and 1 yellow)	2 tablespoons sunflower oil
8 ounces thin green French beans	4 shallots, chopped
3 tablespoons olive oil	2 garlic cloves, chopped
2 skinless, boneless duck breast halves, cut into thin julienne strips	about ½ teaspoon ground dried chili pepper
½ teaspoon salt	1 teaspoon chopped gingerroot
¼ teaspoon freshly ground black pepper	3 bacon slices, chopped
6 anchovies, drained and chopped	4 tablespoons chopped parsley
1 tablespoon white-wine vinegar	2 tablespoons light soy sauce
2 teaspoons sugar	3 ripe tomatoes, skinned and chopped
1 teaspoon lemon juice	6 to 8 ounces rice-stick noodles (the wide-ribbon kind), cooked as described on page 14

1 Prepare the salad vegetables: roast the peppers as described for eggplant on page 49 for 30 to 35 minutes. When cool enough to handle, peel and cut into strips, straining the juice from the peppers and discarding the seeds. Meanwhile, blanch the beans in lightly salted water for 4 minutes. Drain and refresh in cold water; drain again and pat dry.

2 Cook the fried noodles: heat the oil in a wok. Add the shallots, garlic, chili, ginger, and bacon and stir-fry for 5 minutes. Add the parsley and soy sauce and stir-fry for 2 minutes longer. Add the tomatoes and stir-fry for another 2 minutes. Add the noodles and stir until well mixed; adjust the seasoning and turn off the heat.

3 To cook the duck: heat the oil in a skillet. Add the duck strips and stir-fry, stirring frequently, over high heat for 2 minutes. Lower the heat, add the salt, and stir-fry for 2 to 3 minutes longer. Stir in the pepper, anchovies, roasted peppers with their juices, and the beans, cover and leave over medium heat for 1 to 2 minutes. Uncover and stir again for 1 minute. Taste and add the vinegar, sugar, lemon juice, and salt, if necessary.

4 Serve the duck warm on top of the fried noodles, accompanied by a green salad.

Rice noodle salad with spiced ground duck

This can also be made with cellophane noodles and served cold or warm as a first course, or as a light lunch accompanied by a green salad.

Serves 4 as a one-bowl meal, or 8 as a first course

2 tablespoons peanut oil
3 shallots, finely chopped
2 to 4 bird's-eye chilies, finely chopped
4 to 6 skinless, boneless duck breast halves, ground
2½-inch piece of lemongrass stalk, the outer leaves discarded and the soft inner part finely chopped
4 tablespoons chicken stock
3 tablespoons lemon juice

2 tablespoons Thai fish sauce (nam pla, page 141)
2 kaffir lime leaves (page 141), thinly sliced (optional)
8 ounces rice noodles, cooked as described on page 14
2 tablespoons finely chopped scallions
salt and freshly ground black pepper
handful of cilantro leaves, to garnish

❶ Heat the oil in a wok or skillet. Add the shallots and chilies and stir-fry for 2 minutes. Add the ground duck and stir-fry for 2 minutes longer. Add the remaining ingredients, except the noodles, scallions, and cilantro, and increase the heat. Continue stir-fying over high heat until all liquid has been absorbed. Add the scallions and adjust the seasoning.

❷ Reheat the noodles as described on page 16. Put them in a large serving bowl, add the duck mixture, and toss to mix all the ingredients together. Serve immediately.

Soba noodles with peking duck salad

Order whole Peking duck in a Chinese restaurant and the crisp skin will be cut up and served as a first course, wrapped in pancakes smeared with hoisin sauce and accompanied by julienned scallions and cucumber. The meat is stir-fried and served as the main course, with fried rice or noodles. A duck prepared in this way makes an excellent one-dish meal at home. Reserve the wings and carcass for stock and use the back legs in Vietnamese Noodle Soup with Steamed Duck (page 97). Frozen cooked Peking duck is sold in Chinese markets and some supermarkets.

Serves 4 to 6 as first course, or 2 to 3 as a light lunch

1 cooked Peking duck (from an old-style Chinese restaurant, where the ducks are hung in the window) or 1 frozen cooked Peking duck
12 to 16 ounces dried soba noodles, cooked and drained as described on page 14

1 tablespoon light soy sauce
2 to 3 tablespoons hoisin sauce
8 scallions, thinly sliced on an angle
½ cucumber, peeled, seeded, and cut into short sticks
½ teaspoon cayenne pepper (optional)

1 If using frozen duck, allow it to thaw completely, then roast it in an oven heated to 350°F for 45 minutes, starting with the breast upward, turning it over after 15 minutes, and turning it breast-up again after another 15 minutes. Leave it to cool a little, then continue as described in step 3, below.

2 If using a cooked duck from a restaurant kitchen, roast it as above for 30 minutes only, starting with the breast upward, and turning it over after 15 minutes. Leave it to cool a little, then continue as described below.

3 Cut off wings and legs. Reserve the legs for noodle soup and the wings for the stockpot (with the carcass, later). Separate the meat and crisp skin. Slice the meat and cut the skin into julienne strips with a very sharp knife.

4 Reheat the noodles as described on page 16. Toss with half of each of the sauces. Arrange the slices attractively at the side of four plates and stack slices of duck on top. Pile the cucumber and scallions on the other sides and dribble the remaining sauces around. Sprinkle with cayenne pepper, if you like.

Glossary of more unusual ingredients

ANCHOVIES, DRIED Very small dried anchovies (or possibly whitebait) are sold in packages in Asian food stores. They may be labeled *ikan bilis* or *ikan teri*. Buy the ones without heads if you can; if the heads are still on, it is better to remove them.

BAMBOO SHOOTS Don't bother looking for fresh ones. Canned ones (or the baby ones in glass jars) are as good, and far less trouble. Once the can or jar has been opened, unused shoots will keep for up to ten days in the refrigerator, if they are stored in water that is changed daily.

BEANCURD, see tofu

BEAN SPROUTS These can now be bought almost everywhere, but make sure you get fresh, crisp ones. For the sake of appearance, it is worth spending time breaking off and discarding the brownish roots.

BIRD'S-EYE CHILI, see chili

BONITO FLAKES, see *katsuobushi*

CANDLENUTS These are available from many Asian shops, sometimes labeled kemiri. Don't eat them uncooked because they are mildly toxic. Macadamia nuts are a good substitute, and if even these are not to hand, almonds will do.

CHAR SIU Cantonese roasted pork; this can be bought, ready to eat, from many Cantonese restaurants, and in the more traditional ones you will see large pieces of char siu hanging from a rack, usually next to Peking ducks; both have the same glossy dark-brown surface.

CHILI; BIRD'S-EYE The general rule with chilies is that the smallest are the hottest. Bird's-eye chilies (also called bird chilies) are very small, and either bright red or bright green. Color doesn't affect flavor or hotness. Capsaicin, the "hot" constituent of chilies, though completely harmless, can cause discomfort to sensitive areas of skin—eyes, sometimes even fingers, as well as the tongue—so wash your hands after handling chilies. If you get a mouthful of unbearable hotness, cold rice or cool cucumber are soothing; iced water and cold beer are little help. Alcohol can dissolve capsaicin, but you need plenty of it—neat whiskey is said to be effective.

CHILI OIL Giving a mild tang of chili to whatever it's cooked with, versions of this flavored oil are widely available. Commercially produced oil is actually crushed from fresh chili seeds, but you can make your own by slicing four or five dried red chilies very finely and letting them steep for at least a week in about 4 to 6 ounces of oil—any good-quality oil will do, but extra-virgin olive oil is, of course, the best.

CLARIFIED BUTTER This is much the same as Indian ghee, although ghee has more flavor. To clarify butter (remove the solids—sugars and milk protein—it contains), heat it slowly until there is no more froth. The solids are deposited on the bottom of the pan. Strain the liquid butter through fine cheesecloth.

COCONUT MILK This is not the water that, in the tropics, you drink from freshly cut young green nuts. It is a white liquid obtained from the flesh of a mature nut, somewhat rich in saturated fats, but with no cholesterol. It is almost universally used as a cooking medium in coconut-growing countries. I have described, in other books, how to make this *santan* from fresh coconut meat or shredded coconut flakes, but I rarely do this myself nowadays because there are several reliable brands of canned coconut milk sold in Asian food stores, which give results that are almost indistinguishable from fresh *santan*.

DRIED SHRIMP, see shrimp, dried

DRIED ANCHOVIES, see anchovies, dried

FISH SAUCE Often called in the west by its Thai name, *nam pla*, or Vietnamese, *nuoc mam*, this is more or less a liquid version of shrimp paste: a salty, tangy concoction considered essential for savory dishes in many parts of Southeast Asia. It can easily be bought in any Asian food store.

GALANGAL (OR GALINGALE) This is a rhizome, like ginger, although it is pinker and more delicate-looking, and the flavor is quite different—more sour than hot. The Thai name for it is ka. It is fairly easy to find in Asian stores, either fresh or dried and ground. Fresh galangal should be peeled and chopped, like gingerroot.

GINGER JUICE If you aren't all that fond the taste of chopped ginger, use ginger juice to achieve much the same aromatic effect in a dish. To make this: grate fresh gingerroot, leave it for a few minutes in 1 to 2 teaspoons of tepid water, then squeeze the gratings in a garlic crusher or press them through a fine-mesh strainer.

HOISIN SAUCE This Cantonese condiment, used as a marinade and as a sauce for Peking duck, is easily obtainable in Chinese grocery stores and many supermarkets. Its fruity, almost plummy flavor gives little clue to its ingredients, which are largely rice, wheat, soybeans, and sugar.

KAFFIR LIME LEAF These shiny dark-green leaves can be bought, in small packets, in most Thai and other Asian food stores. They impart a mildly bitter, citrus taste to dishes they are cooked with. In some recipes, they are shredded and can be eaten. When left whole, they should be discarded before serving.

KATSUOBUSHI These are shavings of dried bonito fillet, essential for Japanese cooking. The fish is boiled, dried, smoked, and finally cured with a mold similar to the mold used in making soy sauce. *Katsuobushi* can be bought in many Asian stores; it is expensive, but you need to use only a little at a time.

KELP, see *konbu*

KONBU This is the Japanese name for kelp, a broad, flat-leafed species of seaweed used extensively in Japanese kitchens. Like other Japanese ingredients, it is not difficult to find in the west but it is expensive. It is absolutely necessary as the basic flavor of dashi stock (see page 21).

LEMONGRASS Lemongrass hardly needs any introduction as nowadays it is on sale almost everywhere. Most recipes in this book require the tough outer layer or layers of the stalk to be stripped off and discarded. The soft inner part, although rather fibrous, is easily sliced into thin rounds. When cooked as part of a dressing or sauce, it looks attractive, and has a pleasant, slightly lemony flavor.

MIRIN A popular flavoring in Japan, made of fermented steamed glutinous rice mixed with distilled alcohol and matured for between one and two months. This gives it a sweet taste, which it contributes to dishes cooked with it.

MISO This staple of Japanese cooking is a paste of soybeans, rice or barley, and salt fermented with an *Aspergillus* mold; the result is very nutritious, rich in protein, and highly flavored. There are several kinds of miso, but those you will most often find in the west are white miso (made from soybeans and rice) and red miso (soybeans and barley). Miso is sold in sealed plastic packages, but even when opened it will keep in the refrigerator for at least a month.

NAM PLA, see fish sauce

NUOC MAM, see fish sauce

ONIONS, CRISP-FRIED It is easy enough to make your own (page 44), but many stores sell plastic tubs of factory-made fried onions which are just as good. They may also be labeled "fried shallots."

PALM SUGAR This is crystallized from the sweet juice of the flower of the coconut palm, and should be dark red. It is sold in hard blocks, and sometimes appears in the west under its old name of jaggery. To use it, you will need either to grate the block with a coarse grater, or knock a chunk off with a hammer, put it in boiling water, and stir until it dissolves—this can take several minutes.

SAKE The celebrated Japanese rice wine is in fact brewed, not vinified; but to call it rice beer would give quite the wrong impression of this refined drink, the alcohol level of which is roughly that of sherry. Any good average sake that has got as far as the export market is adequate for cooking.

SESAME; ~ OIL, ~ SEED PASTE I use sesame oil as an ingredient for dressings and so on because of its flavor, which is characteristic and very strong; I never use it for frying, where the flavor would interfere with the food. Instructions for making sesame-seed paste are on page 36, but I usually buy the paste.

SHAOHSING WINE This Chinese rice wine is used almost exclusively for cooking. Widely available in Asian stores, it is very easy to identify as, for some reason, it comes in bottles shaped like smaller whisky bottles.

SHOYU, see soy sauce

SHRIMP, DRIED Also sometimes labeled dried prawns, these are sold in Asian stores in packages, already shelled, salted, and roasted. Their flavor is strong, so use them sparingly. In most recipes they first need to be soaked in hot water for 5 to 10 minutes before use.

SHRIMP PASTE This is a very pungent condiment, beloved of Southeast Asian cooks, and I cannot imagine cooking without it. You can buy it, in square 8-ounce blocks, in most Asian food stores, often under the names terasi (Indonesian), blachen or balachan (Malaysian), or ka (Thai). The paste will keep indefinitely, outside the refrigerator, but once the package is opened it should be stored in an airtight container, otherwise the smell will spread through your house.

In cooking, use only very small quantities: about 1 teaspoon, or less than ¼ ounce, is ample for a dish for 4 to 6 people. If a recipe calls for the shrimp paste to be roasted, cut a slice from the block about ¼ inch thick, wrap it loosely in aluminum foil, and roast it in a low oven for 5 minutes. Better still, cut the whole block into slices, spread them in one layer, and wrap them in a double thickness of foil, then roast all of them at one go and store them in a glass jar until you need them.

You can sometimes buy sliced, roasted shrimp paste, but supplies seem to be very intermittent and it is best to roast your own. A slice of shrimp paste can also be broiled or dry-fried in a nonstick skillet (without any foil). The smell is strong, but not unpleasant.

SZECHUAN (OR SICHUAN) PEPPER Szechuan peppercorns, which come from the prickly ash tree, look and taste very different from the black and white peppercorns people are accustomed to in the west. They are now widely available and are essential if you want the real Szechuan flavor, which is usually released by crushing and gently heating the seeds. Also known as anise pepper, fagara, or sansho pepper, it is an essential element in Chinese five-spice powder.

SOY SAUCE; DARK ~, LIGHT ~, SHOYU, TAMARI The soybean is a wonderful vegetable, full of proteins—and, luckily for Asia, these proteins complement those found in rice and make up the full list that the human body requires so, in theory, soybean eaters don't need meat. Unfortunately, much of the bean's nutritional value lies in the parts of it the human body cannot digest. The solution is to ferment the beans with molds that break down these parts and make them available to us when we eat them. This is one reason why Asian cuisines seem to have an obsession with fermented soybean products, although their inventors presumably knew little or nothing about the biochemistry involved—they simply liked the taste.

Among such products is the whole range of soy sauces, tangy and savory, with varying levels of saltiness and sweetness. For the recipes in this book, the important contrast is between light soy, which is salty and thin, and dark soy, which is somewhat sweeter and somewhat thicker and more treacly—although it still pours easily.

The Japanese produce a wide range, but the most easily available is Kikkoman, which you will find in almost any food store and supermarket. I would class this a moderately dark soy. Dutch-made Indonesian-style sauces, usually labeled kecap manis, are thick, heavy, and too sweet for my taste.

Shoyu is simply the Japanese word for soy sauce, but the word is understood, in the west, to mean a particular kind of soy that can usually be found only in Japanese food stores and large Chinese stores. Its flavor is richer and saltier than Kikkoman, and needless to say, it costs more. It is worth the extra money, but if you cannot get it, then Kikkoman, or failing that, any other good-quality soy sauce, will do.

Tamari is a more superior and expensive kind of soy sauce made without wheat; it goes particularly well with sashimi. This, as far as I have observed, is only obtainable in the west in specialist Japanese stores.

TAHINA This sesame-seed paste from the eastern Mediterranean is very similar to that sold in Chinese and other Asian food stores and supermarkets.

TAMARI, see soy sauce

TAMARIND WATER The fruit of the tamarind tree has been popular for many centuries for the pleasantly sour flavor it gives to cooked food. You can buy fresh tamarind, with the flesh and seeds still enclosed in brittle, lumpy pods; but it is more often sold in plastic-wrapped blocks, minus the shells, but with flesh and seeds pressed together into a compact mass. In this book, tamarind is used in the form of tamarind water.

To make 1 cup of tamarind water you need about 1½ ounces of tamarind flesh, broken or cut from the block, or the contents of two tamarind pods. Put the flesh in a bowl and pour a cupful of warm water over. Then press and squeeze the flesh, with your fingers or a spoon, to get the juice out of it and turn the water a rich brown color. When you think you've got as much as you can, strain everything through a strainer and discard the seeds and scraps of flesh. If you make a larger quantity of tamarind water, store it as ice cubes; it will keep in the freezer for up to three months.

Alternatively, put 1 pound of tamarind flesh into a pan with 1¼ quarts of water and bring to a boil. Lower the heat and simmer until the water reduces to half its volume. Strain this, discard the solids, and simmer the water again for 10 minutes; leave the liquid to cool completely. This tamarind water will be about twice as thick and strong-tasting as the kind described above, so dilute it with equal parts of water, unless you prefer the stronger flavor.

TOFU; COTTON ~, FRIED ~, SILKEN ~ As the English name beancurd suggests, this is made from a "milk" extracted from soybeans and then curdled to make a more or less solid block, with the texture and appearance of junket. It is rich in proteins, but has little flavor of its own. However, it picks up and absorbs flavors from the sauces with which it is cooked.

Fresh Chinese-style tofu is available in blocks, weighing about 1 pound, in all Chinese food stores and some Thai stores. Japanese stores, if they sell these, usually call them "Shanghai tofu." Chinese tofu will keep, if submerged in water with the water changed daily, for up to four days in the refrigerator.

Japanese "cotton" and "silken" tofu will keep for a long time as long as the packages remain unopened; once open, they should be used within a few days. "Cotton" is firm enough to slice; "silken" is very soft.

Fried tofu consists of chunks of fresh tofu that have been deep-fried to give them a slightly chewy, but absorbent skin. This adds a more interesting texture to the tofu and helps it to take up the flavors of ingredients with which it is cooked. You can fry your own, but its much more convenient to buy it already fried from a Chinese food store.

VIETNAMESE MINT (RAU RAM) This is not really mint at all, simply another name for one of the two kinds of Thai basil—the kind that has long, pointed green leaves with purple markings. In a Thai store, if you ask for Thai basil you are more likely to get the right plant. In the recipes in this book, I suggest spearmint as a substitute.

VINEGAR; BROWN RICE ~, WHITE-WINE ~ Any Japanese cook will tell you that "real" brown rice vinegar is virtually unobtainable outside Japan, and very expensive there. However, exported branded brown rice vinegars, such as Mitsukan, are widely available and satisfactory for cooking. White-wine vinegar can be found in all supermarkets.

WOOD EARS (OFTEN LABELED "BLACK FUNGUS") These represent one of several types of Chinese dried mushroom (cloud ears are another). They are easy enough to find, although expensive to buy. However, a small quantity goes a long way. They are valued for their texture as much as for their flavor.

YELLOW BEAN SAUCE Yellow (and black) beans, in various forms, can be bought from almost any Asian store. All are variations on salted, fermented soybeans, and they are very salty. Black beans are used when the cook wants the dish to be dark-colored; yellow beans make the sauce just nicely golden.

YOGURT For the recipes in this book, I use whole plain yogurt, but any natural, unflavored yogurt will be satisfactory.

Acknowledgments and Bibliography

I have been learning about noodles practically all my life, so I have many more people to thank than I can name here. I can list only some of those who have helped me, and often given me hospitality as well, during my recent research for this book. Whether you are named or not, please accept my grateful thanks.

In London: Lewis Esson, Mary Evans, Sarah Emery, Gus Filgate and Will Heap, Anne Furniss, Richard Hosking, Deh-Ta Hsiung, Jane Suthering, and Olivier Laudus.

In Vancouver: Nathan Fong, and in Vancouver Island, Sinclair Philip.

In Singapore: at the Four Seasons Hotel, Neil Jacobs, Sam Leong, and Joachin Tan.

As always, my thanks go also to my husband, Roger, and my agent, John McLaughlin, for helping to make the path to publication smoother.

Finally, I acknowledge my debt to the authors of the following books, which I have consulted during my work on noodles:

K. C. Chang (ed.): *Food in Chinese Culture* (Yale, 1977)

Alan Davidson: *The Oxford Companion to Food* (OUP, 1999)

Lesley Downer: *At the Japanese Table* (Chronicle Books, 1993)

Richard Hosking: *The Dictionary of Japanese Food* (Charles Tuttle, 1996; Prospect Books)

Deh-Ta Hsiung: *The Chinese Kitchen* (Kyle Cathie, 1999)

Harold McGee: *On Food and Cooking* (Allen & Unwin, 1984)

Anne Willan: *Complete Guide to Cookery* (Dorling Kindersley, 1989)

Printed in Hong Kong on acid-free paper

98765432

First U.S. Edition

Publishing Director: Anne Furniss
Art Director: Mary Evans
Editor & Project Manager: Lewis Esson
Design Assistant: Sarah Emery
American Editor: Beverley LeBlanc
Food for Photography: Jane Suthering assisted by Olivier Laudus
Styling: Penny Markham
Production: Julie Hadingham

Library of Congress Cataloging-in-Publication Data
Owen, Sri.
     Noodles : the new way / by Sri Owen
    with photographs by Gus Filgate.
        p. cm.
    Includes index.
    ISBN 0-375-50436-2
    1. Cookery (Pasta) 2. Noodles. 3. Cookery,
      Oriental. I. Title.
    TX809.N65 O94 2000
    641.8'22—dc21   00=027532

Index